As a world ranked Pickleball pro and former #1 ranked junior tennis player, I endorse John's book as ideal for **anyone serious about learning the game correctly, having more fun and/or achieving greater tournament success.**
I'm confident you'll see why Callahan Pickleball Academy is known as one of the best. It's **a must-read book written by one of the best teaching professionals.**
> —Joey Farias, Multiple time US Open and National medalist in singles, mixed and men's pro, www.facebook.com/joey.farias.7355

John Callahan has written a great read for those new to the sport of pickleball As well as those who think they already know enough. Everyone can find something here to help their own game.
> —Sarah Ansboury Five-time USAPA National Champion, two-time US Open Pickleball Champion and PPR (Professional Pickleball Registry) educational consultant and lead clinician sarahansboury.com/

PICKLEBALL: TIPS, STRATEGIES, LESSONS AND MYTHS *is a high-quality publication that combines extensive coaching experience with thoughtful analysis. Readers of this book will find practical advice that will help them to be more thoughtful and deliberate on the pickleball court. John's careful approach and personal writing style makes it feel like he's giving you a great private lesson.*
> —Mark Renneson, **Third Shot Sport,** thirdshotsports.com

John is a good friend of mine. He has excellent suggestions for anyone who wants to improve their ability to play Smart Pickleball. His experience as a tennis coach comes handy in how breaks down his views. Good read for any pickleball player.
> —Prem Carnot, **The Pickleball Guru,** PickleballHelp.com

Because I have an extensive collegiate coaching background myself, I took note immediately of John's knowledge, his ability at match analysis and his insight in finding subtle detail changes to affect instant positive change in my game. Pay attention to details in this book and you will learn the game if you are a beginner and you will start to master the game as an experienced player. He is a master at his craft!
> —Teri Clemens, 1997 United States Olympic Committee National Coach of the Year. 7 time NCAA Division III national champion, Head Volleyball Coach: Washington University. Author of **GET WITH IT GIRLS! LIFE IS COMPETITION**

Whether you come from a racket sports background or not, John's book is the definitive guide on understanding the game and getting better at pickleball fast.
> —Rob Nunnery, Former All-Conference D1 Tennis Player and Coach, Current Pro Pickleball Player

... a delightful guide full of important information for those "new to pickleball" players through intermediate players who are serious about becoming more confident and intentional in their overall pickleball game. John is passionate about keeping it fun while sharing pertinent tips and strategies that are essential for mastery towards growing into the pickleball player you want to be.
> —Stephanie Lane, 3-time USAPA National Champion, Gold Medalist U.S. Open, National Director for Pickleball Rocks Clubwear, IPTPA Master Teaching Professional

Getting to know John Callahan, I find him to be passionate, attentive and full of ideas.. It was a pleasure to share my knowledge and fun in his community and with his students. We can all learn something new from those like John, who have taken the time to share their knowledge.
> —Randy Coleman, **USAPA & IFP Ambassador,** Owner of PickleballVoyager.com

In 2017 when I met John my wife and I gave him a lesson in St. Louis. We were astonished seeing a high-level tennis player showing us that he could slow the ball down all the way from the back and then dink and volley like an experienced Pickleball Player. We wish you the best of luck with your book.
> —Coach Matty and Coach Meishen, Pickleballcouple.com

Coach John Callahan is a fantastic player, coach, and author. He is always laughing and smiling. I enjoyed reading his book
PICKLEBALL: TIPS, STRATEGIES, LESSONS AND MYTHS
> —Scott Golden, goldenboypickleball@gmail.com

I have had the privilege of getting to know John over the course of the past year. In that time, I have yet to see John have an "off" day. His level of genuine engagement is there 100% of the time with his students. I have no doubt he will help continue grow pickleball beyond what anyone could imagine. We need more instructors like John Callahan.
> —Andrew Conley, Director of Racquet Sports, Bellerive Country Club

When we began introducing pickleball at the UMSL Recreation and Wellness Center, John's wealth of knowledge helped everyone from beginners to veterans. His lessons were easy to apply and quickly helped all players improve their skills. Regardless your skill level, John's book will help you improve the next time you step on the court.

—Dan Bettmann, Assistant Director of Competitive Sports, UMSL University of Missouri, St. Louis

John and his staff are such an invaluable addition to our clinics. Always offering positive instruction and help for all levels. John is welcoming to all and has inspired many to enjoy the sport and become addicted players.

—Mary W. Klauke, Recreation Specialist, Chesterfield Parks, Recreation & Arts Department

John Callahan and Callahan Pickleball Academy have been instrumental in getting pickleball going in our community. John is professional, patient, hands-on and, to a person, all have enjoyed their introduction to the sport, as well as skill development, under his tutelage. I'm sure you'll gain great insight into the game from this book.

—Miki McKee Koelsch, Recreation Superintendent, City of Webster Groves, MO

John is responsible for much of the growth, enthusiasm and skill advancement in St Louis. He transitioned from a tennis teaching professional to a true pickleball teaching professional. He has taken the initiative to advance his pickleball teaching skills through teaching certifications and by establishing relationships with pros like Sarah Ansboury and Joey Farias. His love for and knowledge of the game makes him uniquely qualified!

—Jenny Pettinga

John Callahan is an elite pickleball teaching professional with a unique ability to successfully communicate his knowledge and strategies to his students. I am blown away with how effectively he translates these tools in his new book, making his skill and charm accessible to all players desiring to improve their game. This book is the perfect "go to" resource for every level to allow players to learn and improve quickly, whether at the 2.5 level or advanced tournament play.

—Julie Goldberg, 4 year USAPA Ambassador, 2 time Southeast Regional Gold Medalist

As a long time tennis player, John taught me with great insight on how to utilize my tennis skills to become a competitive pickleball player very quickly. Whether you a beginner or tournament player or play tennis as I do, this book is for you and you'll see improvement the next time you play.

—Henry Warshaw, C.E.O. Virtual Realty Enterprises

My first impression of John was his positive attitude. When I said I'm the oldest entry in the upcoming 2020 U.S.Open Pickleball Championships in Naples, am ready to spend thousands just to enjoy the big party, so why would I want to pay you even more to bring home a medal? His answer--Harold, give me a chance to work with you, we'll kick some ass! My response: YES! YES! YES! I immediately learned to hit the ball deeper, play better in no-mans land, use a lighter grip and singles strategies. I'm sure John's book will help you too.

—Harold Maness , lifelong sports enthusiast and now at 93 years young, playing pickleball 5 times a week

PICKLEBALL: TIPS, STRATEGIES, LESSONS, & MYTHS

Pickleball:
Tips, Strategies, Lessons, & Myths

*From a Certified Pickleball Professional
& U.S. Open Gold Medal Winner*

JOHN CALLAHAN

CALLAHAN
PICKLEBALL ACADEMY

Manufactured in the United States of America

ISBN: 978-1-7348206-0-7

Cover and interior page design and layout by Stephen Tiano, Book Designer
http://www.tianobookdesign.com
stiano@optonline.net

This book is dedicated to my family, along with a big thank you to my students, facility owners, fellow teaching professionals, and playing partners. Thank you to my two boys, Jack and Joe. I am honored and humbled to be your dad, father, coach, and cheerleader. You have my unconditional love and respect. To our friends, educators, coaches, and leadership at St. Louis University High School (S.L.U.H.): your role in my sons' education, faith, foundation, and life is beyond anything I anticipated. A special thanks to Tracie and to the Stuckey family for their love and encouragement.

CONTENTS

ACKNOWLEDGMENTS

Charlie Cai started as my student in February 2019. He quickly grasped the skills required to improve his game. He is very devoted to pickleball and is fun to teach.

We quickly developed into friends and eventually business partners. Charlie foresaw the tremendous opportunities in pickleball as a fun sport as well as its business potential. He also saw the value, the social good if you will, that pickleball brings to the lives of so many.

Charlie played an important role in publishing this book through his encouragement, process orientation, and financial support. He also has had a very positive impact on my coaching, the development of the Academy, its coming business initiatives, and my life overall. Charlie has become a close friend and respected business partner. Thank you, Charlie.

To my students, thank you for trusting me with your time, game, aspirations, and money. Thank you for coming back over and over for more lessons, thanks for bringing your friends and playing partners, and thanks for all the referrals. Some of you started with me as beginners and just wanted to learn the game correctly. Together, we achieved your goals: more fun with friends and family, improved social and recreational play, playing smarter, and playing safely with less energy. Some of you started with me after winning medals at big tournaments, but had a desire to improve and win at even higher levels. Together, we achieved your goals: you've improved and won medals at even bigger tournaments and at even higher levels. Each of you has made me a better coach. I love watching you excel, grow in many ways, and enjoy this game we cherish together. I will continue to work hard to prepare ways that will help you achieve your goals.

Thank you to the leadership at the St. Louis, Missouri area clubs and facilities that have given me an opportunity to teach pickleball (previously tennis) and have provided year-round homes for Callahan Pickleball Academy since 2017. A special thanks to Dan Apted at Creve Coeur Racquet Club and Dwight Davis Tennis Center, Terry Ward at Frontenac Family of Clubs, Liz Hickox and Bill Reininger of Tower Grove Park, Mary Klauke at Chesterfield Parks, Recreation and Arts, Miki McKee Koelsch at Webster Groves Park and Recreation, Britney Moore at Maryland Heights Park and Recreation, Daniel M. Bettmann at U.M.S.L., Stephan Kruger at Westwood Country Club, Mark Platt of Beginners World Tennis, Alan Douglas of Sunset Country Club, and Andrew Conley and Michael Chase from Bellerive Country Club.

To the teaching pros and professional players who impacted Callahan Pickleball Academy and my life, thank you for your encouragement:

Joey Farias (talented, calm, knowledgeable, encouraging, one of the greatest pickleball players in the world ... what more can I say, check out Joey Farias Pickleball);

Dave Weinbach, one of the pickleball greats ("Hey guys, John is the guy from St. Louis who I told you made 99 out of 100 third shot drops." To which I replied, "Dave, if you want to see your third shot drop, watch me." Check out Dave's videos.);

Three years ago Coach Matty from the Villages ("John, you're the only student I've ever had who was a 4.5 player in five minutes." I took a lesson from Coach Matty in 2017, and five minutes into the lesson, he called me to the net, put his hand on my shoulder, and said, "John, you've found your game." I wiped the tears from my eyes and knew he was right.);

Prem Carnot is a wealth of knowledge, freely shared valuable "coach to coach" advice with me, and loves sharing his insights. Be sure and read the Pickleball Guru's great book, *Smart Pickleball*;

Sarah Ansboury and the entire team at PPR (Professional Pickleball Registry—great program, great instructor, and challenging certification—I'm honored to have achieved the highest level certification.);

Mark Renneson of Third Shot Sports. A delight to teach with and a coaches' coach. Check out Mark's valuable teaching at: ThirdShotSports.com.

Randy Coleman (shout out to Selkirk), Stephanie Lane and KaSandra Marie Gehrke.

Thanks to Sloan Coleman (co-producer and owner of Tiny Little Monsters) and the hundreds of participants for two years of pure fun at The Rockin' Round Robin.

Thank you to my partners at the U.S. Pickleball Open, Tom Ratzki (we won silver in 2019), Jenny Pettinga (we won gold in 2019), and Julie Dyas Goldberg (we didn't win in 2018, but we had fun, and your friendship has been one of the joys in my pickleball life). It was my honor to be on the court with each of you and to compete together.

A very special thank you to Carolyn Sullivan for believing in me; believing in herself; making the Academy so fun, so proud of her tournament performances and so much more. Despite the demands of her interior design company, Carolyn Peterson Design, Carolyn found time to invest in letting the true athlete inside of her come out.

To my friend, Mike Chapin, St. Louis Pickleball teaching pro and
all round great guy, thank you for teaching me how to play
pickleball, for my first paddle, believing in me, and opening
the doors of pickleball to me. To members of the St. Louis,
U.S., and international pickleball ecosystem, thanks for your
encouragement, advice, and friendship.

Some of the Tips, Strategies, Lessons, & Myths you see in this book were
inspired by these friends.

As my students know, private lessons are the most efficient and effective use of time and money if you want to improve your game. However, not
everyone wants to improve, and of those who do want to improve, not everyone is willing to put in the work. Also, not everyone has access to a local
professional pickleball coach. Further, not everyone has the time, money, or
desire to pay for professional lessons. Regardless, this book is for you. Share
and discuss this book with your local teaching professional and playing
partners. Please stay in touch via phone, email, and social media, as we will
continue to offer our tips, strategies, lessons, and myths to help you enjoy
this game we love. Be sure and register your book and your email address
at callahanpickleball.com to receive updates, videos, tips and discounts.
Also, check out our growing online store—phone: (314)474-8400 https://
CallahanPickleball.com/store. Enjoy the journey, and have fun.

A special thanks to our photographers, Danny Reise of Danny Reise
Production and Terrie Rolwes of TR Fine Art Photography/Rolwes Images
and Super Dave Tedoni (friend specializing in pickleball, tennis, photogra-
phy, and real estate). Thanks also to Marc Jorgensen, co-editor, and author
of *Internet Revo;ution: A Generational Story;* and to Stephen Tiano of Tiano
Book Design.

FOREWORD

"John changed my life."

"John is a great coach."

"John makes me believe in myself."

"John is the reason I enjoy pickleball tremendously."

These are only some of the ways that Coach John Callahan's hundreds of students praise him. A talented, local 4.5 pickleball player even printed on his T-shirt, "Doctor—cured my back. John Callahan cured my pickleball."

John's students are a diverse mix. He coaches people who are tough to coach, like CEOs, lawyers, business owners, major developers, and even other coaches from volleyball, skiing, and basketball to golf and tennis! He successfully coaches both people who have a strong foundation in athletic experience and people who don't know how to throw a ball yet!

John's students come from close and far away. Students from all over his home base of St. Louis and as far as Tennessee, and Kansas.—have come to have his lessons. So why is coach John so loved, trusted, and sought after?

I began this life-changing, fun experience with pickleball in late February 2019. At the time, St. Louis was experiencing a long and unbearably cold winter. I didn't know what to expect when I showed up to my first lesson with John. I had played a lot of sports throughout my life, but I never really had a coach. I wanted to make sure that he could deliver on what he charged for the lessons.

After just one lesson, I had learned so much that I decided to take 10 more lessons. Before I even finished those 10 lessons, I added another 10 lessons, worrying that he would be overbooked! Before those 20 lessons were completed, I decided John is such a valuable pickleball coach that I should talk him into writing a coaching book to benefit more pickleball lovers!

Here is how I would describe Coach John:

John is always ready to coach. He is patient. He is aware of his students' abilities and readily able to answer his students' questions with the right lesson for each situation. John has coached people from all levels and all backgrounds.

John is totally committed to creating and maintaining a positive learning environment. He will correct your shots by demonstrating a better way to perform them. He helps to recreate the shots and situations for you, until you really understand what's going on. He won't criticize how you play or put you down in a way that is unproductive. He makes sure you enjoy the game, make friends, and improve your playing skills along the way.

The knowledge of a sport is important for any teacher. John knows pickleball well. He also knows many other sports like tennis, baseball, football, and golf very well, which enables him to break down the barriers that students hit along the way.

I remember how one player was struggling with returning a shot that an opponent smashes over the net. Her reaction was to get scared, lose confidence, and lose focus. John instructed her how to hold her paddle: square and in front of the chest. Right away, she could return the shots and started feeling like she had the confidence to play. Following his lessons, I have seen many people turn their bad playing habits into good habits.

John tracks your growth and progress as a student. He looks you in the eye, explains concepts in a way that is easy to remember, and makes good use of students time. He makes the whole improvement process positive!

The community aspect of pickleball is enormous. John personifies this piece of the game better than anyone I know. You feel like you are part of a family, in a good way! I have made so many more friends playing pickleball than I have in other groups or clubs, friends who I spend time with and get to know on a personal level.

In short, I can confirm, along with hundreds of Coach John's students, that his teachings have had a profound impact on our lives. It has made me a better athlete and improved aspects of my life that I had not expected. I started his lessons with some caution, but looking back on my experiences with him over the past year, I know I would not be nearly the player I am now if I had not participated in his lessons.

When you come across positive changes such as this, it is only natural to want to share them with others. I hope that in this book, you, the reader, will experience positive improvements as a result of reading it.

John is a top-level pickleball coach and certainly among the best in the United States. With the first edition of this book in print, I am sure John will be a top-level pickleball author as well!

—Charlie Cai
Business Partner
Callahan Pickleball Academy

INTRODUCTION

A few years ago, during the early springtime, I was at a public park in St. Louis and came across some folks playing a racquet sport that I didn't recognize. I observed them playing for a few minutes, and it was clear they were having a lot of fun. Their forehand and backhand shots were similar to tennis, which I had played and coached for many years. While tennis was familiar, there was a different and refreshing feel about this sport.

These pickleball players were very gracious and welcoming, something I have found to be quite common among pickleball players. They asked me, "Would you like to play for a bit?" Within minutes, I could play the game well enough to have a great time. Immediately, I was hooked.

That very same day, I went to a sports store and bought some wooden paddles. Several days later, I went back to that same park and played with my two sons. We had a great time discovering this sport and learning the basic elements of serving, moving, and hitting.

A couple of weeks later, I was giving a tennis lesson to a former state tennis champion, who is a gifted and hard-working athlete. She asked me, "John, I really like your coaching methods. Would you be my coach? I want to get back into playing tennis competitively."

When she asked me to be her coach, I stopped and hesitated for a moment. After thinking it over, I simply replied, "I would, but I've fallen in love with pickleball!"

Her response surprised me. "John, you have to meet my friend. He's an ambassador for the pickleball association in St. Louis." I thought this seemed like a fortunate coincidence, so I replied that not only did I want to meet him, but I wanted to meet him tomorrow.

I ended up working quite a bit with Mike Chapin, the pickleball ambassador. In July 2017, I became an official pickleball teaching pro in St. Louis, as I was asked to be the pickleball pro and tennis pro at Tower Grove Park. A few years later, and I have been giving pickleball coaching lessons and clinics almost every day. In this book, I've included my insights over the past 3 years of learning and teaching the tips, strategies, lessons, and myths of pickleball. I hope you find them as useful as my students and I did.

WHY I WROTE
THIS BOOK

I believe that sports have a powerful potential for good in our lives and that there may be a time and a season for different sports depending on our lifestyle.

I grew up playing a lot of sports in the parks of the St. Louis suburbs. Back then, it was easy for kids to play sports in parks. I played football, baseball, tennis, and whatever other sports kids were playing in the parks. By high school, I was focused on tennis. Part of the reason why I focused on tennis was that I got hit in the face by a wild pitch playing baseball. This early injury led to a lifetime of dedication to tennis, which, indirectly, would help me discover the sport of pickleball years later.

My background in playing and coaching competitive tennis for years has helped inform some pickleball observations. Contrary to more established sports, like tennis, there are very few full-time pickleball teaching professionals in the United States. In my home city, St. Louis, I am actually the only coach who holds daily lessons and workshops.

Students will sometimes drive hundreds of miles from neighboring states because I am the most accessible coach to offer personalized instruction. I love it, because I get to play often and see many players' different abilities, styles, challenges and needs. I definitely see a big need for good instruction that players can apply to their own objectives and circumstances.

My early professional career included spending over two decades in the tech industry in the '80s and catching some of the .com boom of the late '90s and 2000s. Some reading this may recall living through those times. What I saw in the tech world then is similar to what I see in the world of pickleball today: pickleball is growing rapidly, the pickleball industry is fragmented, and many players are underserved by the lack of the information and instructions available to them.

In 2019, the *Wall Street Journal* quoted a study released by the Sports & Fitness Industry Association that showed pickleball is one of the fastest growing sports in the country, with over 3 million players.[1] According to the USAPA 2019 pickleball fact sheet, "the known places to play total 6,885 at the end of 2018 represents an increase of 1,016 or approximately 85 new locations per month." Plus each year, the sport grows approximately 10%,[2] which is really amazing growth!

Many new players don't have access to quality instruction. Many also want an inside track on how to improve their game. For pickleball coaching to work, people need a knowledge based approach that adapts to their skill level, athleticism, objectives and personalities.

Given the lack of qualified instructors in pickleball who are also certified, I see this book that you're holding right now as one way to fill this gap, a book that is written clearly to support players who don't have the benefit of a local pickleball coach offering them tailor-made lessons. This book supplies players with many of those same benefits. Regardless of your skill level, you can easily apply the tips, strategies, lessons, and myths you will read. Plus I bet you will have a lot of fun doing it!

Terrie, one of my students, describes my teaching method like this:

"John takes the positive aspects of what you're doing and tweaks them. He gives you encouragement along the way and shows you that you

---

[1] https://www.wsj.com/articles/a-tennis-purist-who-became-a-pickleball-pro-11547899200
[2] https://www.myhighplains.com/entertainment-news/pickleball-is-fastest-growing-sport -among-retirees/

*can do this. I've seen him work with people with no sports background
who experienced big improvements."*

Many of my students also experienced dramatic changes that have positive impacts on other areas of their lives. Carolyn, another one of my students, described her experience:

*"Right away I just knew that this sport was going to change my life.
And it has changed my life. It's given me back my self-confidence after
some major life changes. I enter competitions now, and I've won four
gold medals. There are so many people that I've met; so many positive
stories. I know I'm not an anomaly. I love it."*

Positive stories that have come as a result of playing pickleball are not uncommon. I hear about them all the time. One reason why many people get so much out of pickleball is that it's easy to learn, easy to play, and easy to find courts where you can play seven days a week. Open play sessions also make it easy to play as little or as much as you want and you can go by yourself or with friends.

Carolyn also shared this about pickleball:

*"It's very welcoming. It's a social game and I've met so many great
friends."*

My Coaching Program Is Set Up to Help Students at Their Playing Level

The body of a 65 year old is not going to move like a 25 year old. Differing athletic backgrounds and skills mean that a "one size fits all" lesson doesn't work. If you try to follow pickleball tips online or imitate players at different skill levels, you will:

- likely not focus on the most important fundamentals;
- not play to your strengths efficiently;

- not minimize your weaknesses effectively;
- not have as much fun playing; and
- risk unnecessary bodily injury.

My teaching strategy is built on years of experience and will assist you through improving your game based on your unique abilities and circumstances. Throughout this book, you'll find that my teachings are meant to be adapted based on your current level to improve your athleticism, footwork, swings, and competitive play.

One student shared this:

"The teachings are all based on fun and are very positive. John takes the positive aspects of what you're doing and builds on it. The classes have taken me from a rec player who was having fun and was addicted to pickleball to now playing in tournaments and playing at that advanced level."

The Social Aspect

Another aspect of pickleball that needs to be mentioned is that it is social. The sport offers many opportunities for socializing with others and the social support that comes from meeting new people. This is one of the reasons many people enjoy pickleball and play as often as they do. Terrie put it this way, "It's a competitive sport, but competitive in a fun way."

I really enjoy seeing positive benefits from making friends through pickleball, both for others and myself. This is a major benefit from the sport, and I hope that this social aspect will spread and be shared with more people. Having positive interactions is very important, and it's increasingly harder to find, as our lives become more focused on less personal digital communications. Pickleball is a great change of pace socially.

ADVICE FOR PLAYERS WITH A TENNIS BACKGROUND

"90% of your tennis skills are transferable."

As I mentioned at the beginning of this book, when I first saw pickleball, I could recognize the shots from tennis immediately. The more I learned about pickleball, the more I learned that many of those same skills are transferable. If you can rally the ball, hit a forehand and backhand, and volley, then you can play pickleball in minutes.

It doesn't surprise me at all that among all my students, the single most frequent sports background is tennis. A good 90% of the skills from tennis, such as footwork, swing motion, and balance, transfer to pickleball. It's an easy transition, since pickleball is a bit more forgiving with the shots you make and less demanding with movement.

One major difference between pickleball and tennis is how quickly you can pick up pickleball and have fun playing. In tennis, you typically need many private or group lessons before you get to a point where you actually have good fun playing. In tennis, you need to fine-tune your serves and returns before you can really focus on playing and stop chasing the ball. Contrast this with pickleball, where most players can play the game in only 10 minutes!

My student Terrie described the difference in fun like this:

"I had been a tennis player since I was a kid and have always been competitive and wanting to up my game and play the right

way. I love all sports, but I have never had as much fun as playing pickleball."

Another big difference is that, in pickleball, around 75% of the rallies won come from unforced errors, as opposed to making shots that are outright winners. These statistics are based on my charting of hundreds of matches in my lessons and clinics. This is a different mindset for those coming from a tennis background.

Play tennis from the baseline, same ready position.

Target your shot here, it is the hardest to return.

Here is a key point to consider:

In tennis, you want to get the ball past your opponent. In pickleball, you want to get the ball to the backhand ankle of your opponent or make them reach to hit the ball.

You may be wondering, "Why should I try to get the ball to my opponent's backhand ankle?" This is because this shot is generally the most difficult and uncomfortable one for your opponent to return.

A doubles tennis court is over three times greater in size than a pickleball court. Since a pickleball court is smaller than a tennis court, it is tough to hit the ball by your opponent and still keep the ball in the court. So, ideally, you want to get the ball to your opponents' backhand ankle. If you can do this, they will either:

A) hit back a ball that is easier for you to return, or
B) hit the ball into the net or out of bounds.

In tennis, hitting the ball past your opponent with a high-speed or strong force is a big part of scoring points. It's harder to do that in pickleball because the court is much smaller and a hard hit pickleball travels slower than a tennis ball. Placement is more important than power.

Terrie put it this way:

"Tennis is a power game, gripping the racquet tightly, squatting and thinking how you are going to power that ball back."

In pickleball, rallies are most often won differently. Points in pickleball come from avoiding risky moves and low percentage shots. You set up the rally by getting the ball to a spot where your opponent is likely to make an unforced error or give you an attackable ball.

Often, the best choice is not making some magical hit, but just getting the ball over the net. In the sections on **MY STUDENTS' FAVORITE LESSONS**, I demonstrate how to use these tactics in the different scenarios you'll encounter.

Why You Need to Have a Pickleball Epiphany

Tennis and other racquet sports give players a great foundation to build upon. However, this foundation is not enough to be a great pickleball player. I've learned from working with many players that you need to have a "pickleball epiphany."

A "pickleball epiphany" is that moment where you unlearn the habits and ideas from tennis, or another sport, and wake up to the strategy and mindset of pickleball. I've seen many players play pickleball for years before realizing they were missing this fundamental aspect.

Terrie shared the following about making her switch from tennis to pickleball:

> *"The majority of players in rec play or open play are playing tennis or racquetball but on a pickleball court and with pickleball paddles. I used to run around the court and just be exhausted. John taught me how to hit the ball out in front of your body and how to avoid the whipping tennis motion. How to take a breath, relax, and play strategically."*

Now I don't share these ideas to be critical in any way. As a tennis player myself, I have also had to learn these lessons. Here are five factors that tennis players need to internalize:

1 *Putting Spin on the Ball*

Starting out, if you try to put a spin on the pickleball, you will never improve. Tennis and racquetball both have racquets made of strings with a tension that produces a strong bounce for the ball. The tennis ball compresses, and the tennis racquet's strings grip the ball, enabling spin. Pickleball paddles are hard, and the ball doesn't compress. This combination makes putting spin on the ball difficult, resulting in unforced errors and losing the rally.

Once your playing level gets more advanced, as we will discuss later, there are some situations for spin to be used. But starting out, don't try to put spin on the ball. It will slow your improvement and neutralize your skill set, plus you'll have less fun playing.

2 Hard Paddle, Hard Ball

The hard pickleball paddle hits differently than the strings on other racquet sports' paddles. The good part is that the pickleball paddle is less likely to overreact to your hits.

The pickleball ball is made of a hardened plastic material. It is much less bouncy than a tennis ball. The upside of having a less bouncy ball is that it is more predictable and easier to control. A small change in angle won't necessarily make the ball fly way out of bounds as in tennis.

Adapting to a hard paddle will take some time. Terrie mentioned this about using the different paddles:

> "Let your paddle do the job. In tennis, you manipulate the racquet and put power into it. In pickleball, you let the paddle hit the sweet spot, and it's all good."

3 Lower Net and Higher Margin for Error

The net is lower in pickleball in the middle than the sidelines. I have noticed that current and former tennis players don't realize how a lower net changes the game dynamics. The lower net moves the ideal spot of both where you should hit and how high you need to clear the net. In pickleball, you should always clear the net with plenty of room for a higher margin of error.

The net is 2" higher at the sideline, the ball does not go over.

The net is 2" lower in the middle, the ball now goes over.

4 Hit the Ball Down the Middle, Not Down the Sides

Because you are playing on a smaller court in pickleball and most points come from unforced errors, you don't need to hit the ball down the lines like in tennis. Tennis conditions players to aim for the corners, and with a big court and lots of space, that's a good strategy. We will discuss the ins and outs of pickleball strategy and positioning in more detail in the sections on **MY STUDENTS' FAVORITE LESSONS**.

For now, remember that you will have to unlearn this habit. Hit the ball down the middle, and don't aim to hit the ball within inches of the sideline. It's not worth the risk of hitting the ball out of bounds.

One in, one out, play it safe, hit several feet inside sideline.

5 You Must Learn to Dink

The technique for hitting a "dink" and the strategy behind it are crucial to intermediate and advanced play. A dink is similar to a tennis drop shot hit when you are close to the net. It's a foreign concept to most players, including those with a background in tennis. A dink is a upward light hit, made when you're up at the kitchen line (the non-volley zone line), which is intended to go over the net and land near the feet of your opponent and in their kitchen (in the non-volley area), forcing them to hit up on the ball. Instead of dinking when the ball is below the net, tennis players often hit the ball hard and into the net, hard and out of bounds or hard and up, enabling their opponent to attack their ill-conceived shot. In short, to progress quicker and have more fun, you must learn when, why and how to Dink as soon as possible.

My student Carolyn shared a story about learning to make the dink shot:

"The dink shot is not a hard concept. What's hard is your patience. In tennis, you accelerate through the ball. In pickleball, you do everything you can to slow the ball down. It's important to master this slowing down process to hit the dink correctly. I overcame this over time through patience."

6 Spatial Dimensions

A tennis doubles court is three times bigger than a pickleball court. On such a larger court, it's not hard to see the open space. On a pickleball court, you need to use more planning to create and open up space or, as I call them, gaps. In the sections on **MY STUDENTS' FAVORITE LESSONS**, I will explain what you need to do to create the gap, see the gap, and hit the gap.

When I first saw people playing pickleball in the park, I could recognize the strokes from tennis. When you hit ground strokes and a service return in pickleball, the patterns are in fact quite similar to tennis. But remember this, as you move forward from the baseline through the transition area (or no man's land) to position yourself at the kitchen (the non-volley zone), this is when you start to really play pickleball.

We will go into all of this in much more detail in **MY STUDENTS' FAVORITE LESSONS**.

In Summary

Any current or former tennis player who takes into account the above six "pickleball epiphany" concepts will be in a great position to excel in pickleball. I really believe that if you do this by having that "pickleball epiphany," you can move from playing at a beginner level to an intermediate level within a short period of time, depending, of course, on how often you practice and your lesson regime. Please note that I did not mention how often you play. Practice and lessons are key to rapid improvement, and I have seen such positive changes in many new players who start with an emphasis on lessons and practice.

ADVICE FOR PLAYERS WITH LITTLE OR NO SPORTS BACKGROUND

"If you can move your feet and have hand-eye coordination, you can play within seven minutes."

I have seen people with a limited sports background get so much out of pickleball. Carolyn is one student who has made major improvements with very little sports experience:

> *"I never played a sport with the exception of Junior High Volleyball. So, I always wondered if I could have been athletic. I got introduced to pickleball, played for a couple weeks and was horrible. I took some lessons and my game started to improve. It has really helped me become athletic."*

You don't have to be a world-class athlete or in the best shape of your life to have fun and compete at pickleball. The sport attracts people from all kinds of athletic experiences and backgrounds.

Like any sport, to be good at pickleball, you will need to give it some effort and practice, beyond just hitting it around or playing occasionally. There is a quote from Pope John Paul that I like to share with people, "Be not afraid," so don't be afraid to get started!

What also makes pickleball special is how the dynamics of the way it's played make it so much easier to have a good time while improving your game. That's why it's so enjoyable for me to coach lessons and play every day.

My student Charlie shared this story about a fellow student:

"I have seen students who are very successful in their professional life who have limited sports background. One player started playing a bit awkwardly at first. John lessons helped a lot with his blocking, serving, and movement. Within a couple months he made tremendous progress. He started to love the sport, and now he brings his son out to play."

As a player, you should always try to leverage whatever sports or athletic background you have. Don't let anyone put you in a pickleball box or a one-size-fits-all approach. Many skills from other sports can be applied to pickleball. My approach is: why would you want to get rid of the skills you already have?

You can keep what you have learned from prior athletic experiences, no matter how small. And I can show you how to best fit these skills into pickleball.

When I was living in San Francisco, it was during the early voicemail and voice processing industry boom of the mid '80s to early '90s. My job was very competitive and demanding. Around this time, I fell in with a group of other professionals whose objective was training to play U.S.T.A. 5.0 tennis on a national level. This required hours of training every day.

To pull this off required that you either A) quit your job, or B) be in a position that would allow for having a lot of control over your day. The training paid off. I, and others I played with, competed successfully at regional and national competitive events, including U.S.T.A. 5.0 national championships.

You may be interested in competing at local or national level pickleball events, or you may just be looking to up your game and meet new friends. Both goals are totally worth it. But regardless of the level of play you are aiming for, you need to know the essentials and invest your time. My lessons and techniques are designed to be adapted to help you get you there.

Online Learning

There are many videos and other training material available online. But it is important to remember that the shots you are seeing at a national championship game are not necessarily the shots that everyone can do. Copying their moves will also not help you make the right shot at the right time. Along their journey to championships, those champions started with consistent high percentage pickleball shots. They focused on reducing unforced errors and strategic shot selection. You should do the same.

One reason I love coaching, and why I wrote this book, is helping students find and capitalize on their strengths and weaknesses. Lessons should be structured around your objectives, playing style, and ability. Just watching an online video will not necessarily make you capable of emulating that same performance. This can only be done through lots of practice, discernment, and observation while playing. A coach with experience, and a professional approach is how you can best focus your physical abilities to see the improvements you want.

Social Side of Pickleball

Contrasting the sport with tennis, Carolyn observed:

> *"Tennis is different in that you set a time, show up, and play. In pickleball, you show up but don't need a partner. The partner is not the same every time. You show up, play, make friends. Pickleball is a very social game. I've met so many good people."*

Open Play: The Playground of Beginners, Amateurs, and Recreational Players

Open play is a big part of the social fabric of pickleball. In many cities, you can find places with courts available daily. These are usually open for several hours, often between 9 a.m. and 3 p.m., where people can just show up, play pickleball, and meet new friends. The great thing is you don't need pre-arranged games with pickleball. Open play is the friendly and fun foundation of the sport.

As the name implies, open play is all about the social openness that is so common with pickleball players everywhere. All levels of play are welcome, from the amateur to the expert.

Open play is like being a kid on a playground again. Just like when you were a kid, it's hopefully fairly easy to make new friends and to learn new things.

However, despite the overall friendliness and welcoming nature of most pickleball players, there are some who don't want to play with players below "their level," and some, despite their scant knowledge, are prone to "volunteering their coaching." Forget about the former, be wary of the latter, and move on to the goal: fun.

PICKLEBALL BASICS

In this chapter, we'll review some of the fundamentals required to play pickleball. It also includes some of the basic shots that we'll cover before moving on to more advanced techniques.

The Handshake Grip

The handshake grip is the most effective paddle grip. To make the grip, you shake hands with the paddle making a V between your thumb and forefinger. The V should be in the middle of the skinny side of the grip, pointing toward the upper edge of the paddle. You hold the paddle firmly in your palm, and then with your fingers, secure it gently (about a 3 to 4 on a scale of 1 to 10 in tightness).

You can use this grip throughout the game on all shots. It's easy to do and will give you the best consistent control.

The Serve

Shake hands with the paddle, paddle becomes extension of your hand.

"V" between your thumb and forefinger runs along the skinny side of the handle.

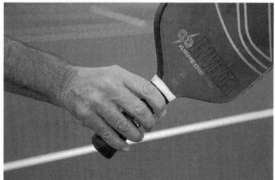

Hold the paddle in your hand, not in your fingers.

Welcome to Your "Happy Serve."

I say that because I want you to enjoy your serve, to feel confident hitting it and to consistently get the ball into the back ⅓ of the correct service box.

Given that as our objective, I've simplified the serving motion. I've had far too many students, some great athletes; others not so much who have spent months or years playing with a poor serve or for some inexplicable reasons find themselves not being able to serve well for a period of time (in golf, they call it the "yips").

Some students came to me with poor motions, poor ball tosses, overly bent knees, hunched backs, wildly swinging arms, never watching the ball, never looking at the target, excessive follow throughs or no follow through at all ... you name it. They may not even realize how many serves they miss. They may not even realize how many serves they get in are actually so poor they have little chance to win a point. They may not even realize how bad they look, and how injury prone they are and how much wasted energy their service motion causes. Often, they dread having to serve.

I want you to look forward to serving, to be confident serving and to get the ball where it's supposed to go. All this with minimal effort and a motion that won't break down under pressure. I know there are many ways to serve. This is our way and I encourage you to try it.

Stand behind the baseline at a 45 degree angle to the correct service box so that a line from your back big toe to your front big toe (the one closest to the baseline) would continue into the middle of the correct service box. Imagine a line of markers showing you the target line from your feet to your target in the back $\frac{1}{3}$ of the service box. Stick your arms straight out so that the front facing arm points to the correct service box. If both the line at your feet and your arms aren't parallel and don't point to the target, readjust until they do. Now, look at the target.

 Now, swing the paddle alongside the front of your body with the paddle face facing the target. Notice I said alongside the front of your body, don't swing across your body and don't swing behind your body. At no time should the paddle be behind your hip during your backswing or wrapped around your body during your follow through. At no time should the paddle face not be facing the target ... said another way, at all times, the paddle face should be facing the target. Your paddle will be angled down during the backswing and angled slightly up towards the target as you swing forward.

Now, simply put the ball in the way of the paddle motion and hit through the ball. Hold the ball slightly in front of your front foot and toss it gently up a few inches or let it drop down a few inches and let the paddle hit the ball. It's your choice to toss it up gently or drop it. The key with the toss is consistency. Make contact near the lower back of the ball with a low to high motion so you create a high enough trajectory (without being a high lob) that your ball easily clears the net and lands in the back ⅓ of the service box. You do

A line from back to front foot points to the target. *Note:* The yardstick and markers point to target.

Front arm points to target, back arm at 180 degrees.

Your target is middle deep, back one-third of service box.

Swing the paddle alongside the front of your body.

Finishing the swing in front of your body.

Put the ball in the way of the paddle and hit with a low to high motion.

Common mistake: Don't hit the ball too far in front of you.

Common mistake: Don't hit the ball too low in front of you.

Common mistake: Don't hit the ball close to your back hip.

Common mistake: Don't hit the ball side arm or above your belly button.

not need to put a lot of pace on the ball. In fact, there's a case to be made that if you put a lot of pace on the ball, you've made it easier for your opponent to return your serve. You don't have to try to consciously hit the ball, because you've moved the ball into the path that the paddle is going anyway. Just look at the ball and the paddle will hit it. The accompanying photos show how to hit it and what most commons mistakes to avoid. Remember the rules, ball hit below the belly button in an upward motion and the paddle must be below the wrist.

Should I step? You can step if you want to step. Stepping doesn't matter as much as ensuring you transfer your weight from back foot to front foot. Also, don't leave your back foot on the ground. As you hit the ball and follow through to the target, your back hip comes around, your back foot turns on its toes and shows it sole and your belly button ends up facing the target.

Check out our serving drills in the **MY FAVORITE DRILLS** chapter.

Welcome to your "Happy Serve." Enjoy the journey to a consistent, effective and efficient serve.

Ground strokes: Overview

I encourage my students who have played any racket sport before, to start hitting ground strokes by using the same forehand or backhand to which they are accustomed. Yes, I tell them to start out by hitting their forehands and backhands however they want. After all, the initial objective is to have fun, get the ball over the net and to experience quick success. If they're not hitting the ball over the net and generally towards their target then I recommend slight modifications to their ground stroke motion. Most likely they are not hitting low to high, their paddle face isn't open at contact or they're trying to put too much spin on the ball. I suggest small changes to immediately improve their consistency so rallies last longer and they have more fun.

Once they're at least getting the ball over the net, it's time to take a deeper look into the forehand and backhand. As you may know a groundstroke is either a forehand or backhand shot that is hit after the ball bounces. It is typically hit from at or near the baseline. The success of your ground strokes are most often determined by: accuracy, consistency, speed, net clearance, trajectory, your court position and your opponents' court positions. Ideally, the ground stroke will only be used once on your serve return as I expect you to be advancing towards the kitchen line after the shot.

Ground stroke: Forehand

Assumptions:

For our purposes, we'll assume you're within a foot or two of the baseline. We'll also assume you are attempting to hit the ball over the net with a high margin of error, near the centerline and in the back 1/3 of the court. The forehand we're discussing here is not a third shot drop shot, it is a forehand drive. The forehand is usually the most powerful, accurate and consistent shot. That is why it is so often used on the service return or other shots near the baseline.

Face the ball:

Start out by facing the ball. Facing the ball makes the ball flight easier for you to see and to judge. It also makes the ball easier to hit. In other words if your opponent hitting the ball (or serving) is on the even side and you are on your even side, turn slightly (up to 45 degrees) so you are looking directly at them. If your opponent who is hitting the ball is on the even side and you are on your odd side, you simply face forward as you're directly across the net from each other. By not facing the ball, you make the ball flight more difficult to judge and the ball more difficult to hit accurately.

The Grip:

The preferred grip is the handshake grip (aka the Continental). For more detail on the grip, please *see* **PICKLEBALL BASICS**: **Handshake Grip** (page 37).

Move Towards the Ball:

Once you see where the ball is headed, move towards the ball. Most likely this will accomplished by making lateral moves along the baseline. However, if your opponent's shot (or serve) is short versus deep in the court; you'll need to move in to hit it. If your opponent's shots are consistently short, then step in a few feet and get into your ready position.

Closed Stance:

I prefer a "closed stance" (meaning your shoulders, chest, hips and feet are perpendicular to the net) versus the "open stance" (meaning your shoulders, chest, hips and feet are facing the net) when hitting a forehand. Your stance is not so closed that it feels restrictive and doesn't allow the hips to easily open and turn towards the target. Also, your stance is not so open that you're unable to transfer your weight forward and therefore can only generate power by swinging your arm harder. Think of the closed stance much like a baseball hitters stance at

Closed stance like hitting a baseball. Go Cards!

the plate or a golfers stance as preparing to hit the ball off the tee box. The non-paddle shoulder and corresponding foot are closer to the net and pointed towards the sideline. If you're right handed, this means your right foot and right shoulder are back, closer to the baseline. A line from your back foot to your front foot and the line from your back shoulder to your front shoulder should point to the target.

Backswing:

Using a shoulder and hip turn, bring the paddle back anywhere from 12:00 to 3:00 in relation to your back knee. Your elbow should be bent slightly comfortably and should be closer than farther from your body. Your non-paddle shoulder should be closer to the net. Please don't go beyond 3:00 on your backswing as that puts the paddle behind your hip forcing you to swing needlessly from behind your body and likely across your body instead of in front of it. Also, please avoid the big looping backswing common with tennis players. You don't have the time for the loop and it is unnecessary to prepare to hit the ball.

Weight Transfer:

As you prepare to hit the ball, your weight will initially be more on your back foot. As you rotate your body and swing the paddle you will transfer your weight to your front foot. It is important to remain in balance throughout the entire forehand motion (including the ready position, swing and follow-through).

Rotate and Finish Your Shot:

Once you're in the ready position and your weight is on your back foot you are ready to take your shot. Rotate your upper body forwards and open your hips toward the target. Swing the paddle alongside the front of your body with a low to high motion. End your follow through with the paddle tip facing your target. A simple, fluid and pendulum swing is all you need. In addition to increasing the likelihood of a solid hit, you'll now be in a ready position to move forward and prepare for the next shot.

Impact Zone:

By setting up correctly in the closed stance, you increase the size of your impact zone. Your impact zone is the area where you can hit (impact) the ball towards your target with consistency and minimal energy. The impact zone is generally between the inside of your back knee and extends through the center of your body to your front foot. Your impact zone should be a foot or two long. You don't want to make contact with the ball near your back hip and you don't want to have to reach out too far over your front foot to hit the ball. At either extreme you lose accuracy and waste energy. Throughout the impact zone you want your paddle face to be facing the target. In fact, you want your paddle face to be facing the target slightly before, during and slightly after you swing through the impact zone. Attempt to make contact with the ball at a height somewhere between your knees and your waist. Often that means you'll have to move to the ball to avoid reaching to hit the ball.

Avoid Reaching:

Speaking of reaching, there are two types or reaching. One is reaching out further from your body to hit the ball because you are too far away from the ball. The other is reaching down to hit the ball. Both have negative consequences. Reaching should always be minimized. Move your feet and body closer to the ball so you don't have to reach out too far to hit the ball. Bend your knees and bring your head closer to the paddle so you are not reaching down too far to hit the ball. Remember, either type of extreme reach reduces the size of your impact zone and causes inaccuracy, inconsistency and weak hits. So remember, move closer to the ball to improve your accuracy, consistency and solid ball striking.

Watch the ball:

Watch the ball intently. Watch the ball with purpose. Keep your head down and eyes closer to the paddle. Watch the ball hit the sweet spot. Keep your eyes and head down even after the ball leaves your paddle and your paddle leaves the impact zone.

Low to High Motion:

Swinging from slightly below the ball to above the ball imparts natural top spin on the ball, helping it get over the net and drop at your desired target. The more you start your swing with the paddle lower (below the ball) and finish above the ball, the more natural top spin you impart. Flipping your wrist or overly bending your elbow dramatically reduces consistency, accuracy and power.

Follow-through:

Your follow through is shorter than in tennis. Finish with your paddle tip pointing to the target. Please do not follow through all the way to the other side of your body or above your non-paddle shoulder. At the end of your follow-through, your shoulders and hips will have turned to face your target. Your belly button is also facing the target. Your back foot has turned up on its toe so the sole of your shoe is showing and pointing backwards. Your weight has been transferred from your back foot to your front foot.

Hit Your Fave Shot:

Given a choice, and you almost always have a choice, hit your strongest shot. Hit your fave, whether it is a forehand and backhand. If the ball is slightly to your weaker shot, simply run around it and get into your ready position as early as you can. You may have up to 44 feet to get ready so stay calm and get in position as early as you can. For most of my students, the forehand is the preferred ground stroke and it is the shot most often used to hit the service return. For pictures of a forehand in balance, please *see* **MY STUDENTS FAVORITE LESSONS 15: Be Balanced Before, During and After the Shot**.

Ready position facing the ball

Backswing complete, starting weight transfer

Follow through to target, head stays down and weight transfer complete

Ground stroke: Backhand:

Please don't be intimidated by a backhand shot. The fundamentals are similar to the forehand.

The main difference is: when you turn your shoulders and hips it is now the paddle shoulder that is closest to the net (remember, the non-paddle shoulder is closer to the net on the forehand) as you await the ball your opponent hit to the non-paddle side of your body. Also, your impact zone is slightly forward of where it is on your forehand.

Look here for more help with your forehand and backhand:

PICKLEBALL BASICS: **Handshake Grip** (page 37)

PICKLEBALL BASICS: **Footwork** (page 50)

PICKLEBALL BASICS: **Firm Wrist** (page 53)

PICKLEBALL BASICS: **Steady Heady** (page 54)

MY STUDENTS FAVORITE LESSONS:

#1 Just Don't Miss

#10: Running while hitting violation

#11 Minimalist Movement

#12 Your Ready Positon is determined by your court location

#15 Be Balanced Before, During and After the Shot

#18 I just want to look good

#21 Low Percentage Shots to Avoid

#24 Hit Through the Ball, Not At IT

#30 The Game Is More Fun When Rallies Last Longer

#31 It's Not "Fire, Ready, Aim"

10 DANGEROUS MYTHS:

 #4 Hit your return of serve hard

#5 Hit the Ball as Close to the Top of the Net as You Can

#9 Just Hit it Hard or Just Hit it Soft

And if you use our warm up (*See* **TIPS FOR WARMING OP**), you'll have hit at least 30 forehands and backhands before you start playing.

SERVICE RETURN

Basics:

Please apply all the basics of the forehand and backhand to your service return. Perhaps more important than any other shot, you should have a well thought out target and ball trajectory in mind before you hit the service return.

Target & Trajectory:

Keep your service returns deep as it gives you more time to get towards the kitchen line and makes your opponents third shot more challenging. Hit a lofty return as opposed to a low hard shot as this gives you even more time to move towards the kitchen line and makes your opponents third shot even more challenging. I recommend hitting every service return deep and down the middle until your consistency is such that you can target an opponent's backhand and not hit the ball out of bounds (deep or wide) or short. Keeping your opponents deep after they serve puts you in the best position to win the rally. Error on the side of hitting high percentage service returns until your accuracy improves.

Move Forward Immediately, Every time:

Remember, you're coming in immediately after you hit your service return. You're then stopping once your opponent starts their backswing. Please note that it is better to be in the correct ready position at a bad court position than not to be ready in a more advantageous court position.

Hit your Fave:

Given a choice, and you almost always have a choice, hit your service return with your fave (your strongest shot), be it your forehand or backhand. If the ball is slightly to your weaker shot, simply run around it and get into your ready position as early as you can. In fact, adjust where you stand on the baseline for your service return ready position so you are likely to get more balls hit to your fave shot. You will see the ball flight from 44 feet away, so you have time to get into your ready position and even run around a shot if desired. Maintaining your balance is so important: *please see* **MY STU-DENTS FAVORITE LESSONS 15: Be Balanced Before, During and After the Shot**.

Look here for more help:

There are many tips, strategies, lessons and myths included in this book that you can use to improve your service return. To save you time, here are the references to help you improve your service return:

PICKLEBALL BASICS: **Handshake Grip** (page 37).

PICKLEBALL BASICS: **Footwork** (page 50)

PICKLEBALL BASICS: **Firm Wrist** (page 53)

PICKLEBALL BASICS: **Steady Heady** (page 54)

My Students Favorite Lessons:

#1 Just Don't Miss

#11 Minimalist Movement

#12 Who Wants To Run

#13 Your Ready Position at the Baseline

#15 Be Balanced Before, During and After the Shot

#24 Hit Through the Ball, Not At IT

#30 The Game Is More Fun When Rallies Last Longer

#31 It's Not "Fire, Ready, Aim"

10 Dangerous Myths:

#4 Hit your return of serve hard

#5 Hit the Ball as Close to the Top of the Net as You Can

#9 Just Hit it Hard or Just Hit it Soft

Hitting Drills:

Two-Returns

Footwork Drills

Ready position on the service return	Service return backswing complete, starting weight transfer	Service return follow through to target, head stays down and weight transfer complete

Footwork

The one thing I'll say initially about the footwork in pickleball and footwork in general is that you most often can't make your second step and subsequent steps much faster. You can, however, make your first step faster.

The trick to this is keeping an eye on the flight of the ball coming toward you and/or your opponent's paddle from across the net. You can spot where the ball will be coming. Using this, you can anticipate the direction you will need to step to make the hit that you will need to make. Seeing the ball at up to 44 feet away will allow you to take that first step sooner.

Some general guidelines for improving your footwork:

1. Small steps are better when you are near the ball, since those steps are easier to control and better balanced. Use longer steps first, and then small steps as you get closer to the ball.
2. Once you are in place, in balance and ready to hit the ball, always be moving toward, or stepping toward, the target (such as the kitchen) when possible.
3. To avoid reaching for the ball, take a step toward the ball and get into the ready position, instead of reaching and swinging toward the target with your paddle facing the target.
4. Keep your feet under your body. This will maintain balance and high probability shots.
5. Remember to transfer your weight from back to front to avoid getting out of balance. Being off balance even a little can mess up the angle of your shot.

Body Positioning

In between every shot, you should be moving toward the kitchen, as permitted. Maybe you'll get halfway to the kitchen or maybe you get all the way there. The important thing is to be moving toward the kitchen. Good players stop and get into a ready position when their opponent starts their backswing. Beginners run mindlessly to the kitchen without regard to when their opponent may hit the ball.

Your ready position is more important than your court position. Remember this as you move around the court. A lot of players do not get into the ready position early enough. Don't sacrifice your readiness for a better court position—it's not worth it!

Firm Wrist

Don't flip your wrist. This will mess with the angle of your shot. Keep your wrist firm. The ball will go to where your paddle face is going when your wrist is firm. When you flip your wrist, your timing must be absolutely 100% perfect or the ball will not go where you want it to go. That's why so few, if any, good players flip their wrist. So keep your wrist firm and your game will improve immediately.

Steady Heady

Head down, eyes on ball, putted ball lands in cup.

Head raised, eyes not on ball, putter misses ball.

This concept is borrowed from golf. It boils down to this simple concept: don't raise your head before you hit the ball.

The reason for this is that raising your head, even for a split second before you hit the ball, impacts the direction your shot will take. Keep your head steady and eyes on the ball as you make your shot. This is a very important habit to develop. Even a small change in movement in your head can affect the angle and direction of your shot.

We will revisit this concept to understand how it applies to different game situations in the sections on **MY STUDENTS' FAVORITE LESSONS**.

Kitchen (Non-Volley Zone) Shot: The 'Dink' Shot Explained

The "dink" is one of those words you hear a lot in pickleball and no other sport. It's a shot that you'll want to use very often.

Some basics for the dink shot are:

1. The dink is a light hit arching safely over the net, typically hit from just behind or just inside your kitchen (non-volley zone), and then bouncing in your opponents' kitchen.
2. You want to hit the dink from a low position to a high position while also ensuring you clear the net with a high margin of error.
3. It's best to use a dink to target an opponent's backhand or body. There'll be more on this in the section on **MY FAVORITE DRILLS**.

The perfect paddle angle for a soft dink when hitting a low ball.

The main purpose of the dink is to force your opponent to hit up on the ball. When your dink causes your opponents to reach for the ball or shift their body position in a way that makes it hard for them to return your shot or to return to their ready position, you hit a good dink! A good dink leaves your opponent off balance and out of position for your next shot.

Making it harder for your opponent to make a good shot will set you up to make a much better shot, potentially a winner.

Here is a breakdown on how to ideally use the dink:

1. You dink the ball to a spot that is difficult for your opponent to cover (e.g., low backhand).
2. Your opponent rushes, cross steps or reaches to return the dink.
3. Your opponent hits back a weak high shot, which is easily attackable.
4. You attack the ball, hitting the ball back to a gap in your opponent's court.
5. The ball lands out of your opponent's range, and you win the rally!

Perfecting the art of the dink takes practice. After learning to serve, to hit a forehand, to volley, and to use good footwork, hitting the dink is one of the most essential skills to playing pickleball at an intermediate or advanced level.

For that reason, players should try hitting dinks when they first start playing. Practice dinking every time you play and make dinking part of your warmup. There's more on this in the section on **TIPS FOR WARMING UP**. Don't expect to perfect it right away—it will take time.

My student Terrie said this:

"The dink came easy quite frankly, but there's an art to it. It's the most fun part of the game. I love it, and when you can attack it, it's even better. But the hard part is the variables of where you are playing. If it's indoors, outdoors, or with wind, all these factors make it challenging."

Don't be discouraged if you don't perfect the dink right away. My student Carolyn, who has become very successful competing in tournaments, said this about the dink:

"In competition it is still something I'm always working on. But to really finesse the dink shot, it took me a good nine months."

One mistake people make is to mindlessly dink. To avoid this, I suggest using a little strategy in your approach. You can check out the drills called **Dink, Three by Three** and **Dink, Volley, Attack** in the chapter MY FAVORITE DRILLS.

> **PRO TIP**   Players expecting to get to an intermediate or higher level of play are expected to be able to dink to three target areas with a 95% accuracy.

The Volley

A volley is hitting the ball out of the air back to your opponent without waiting for the ball to bounce. Volleying is one of the core elements of pickleball that makes it so much fun. Because we use hard paddles, the speed of the volley tends to be a bit slower than other racquet sports. However, since we are playing on a smaller court, there is a lot of rapid fire volleying.

General Tips on Volleying

In hitting volley shots back and forth, I advise students to hit the ball directly out of the air and as soon as you can without overreaching and losing your balance. The reason for this is hitting the ball straight out of the air, not waiting for it to bounce, will take time away from your opponent to respond to your hit. Get time on your side.

Hit the volley. Waiting for the ball to bounce can force you to lose some momentum. Remember that when using the volley, you may not necessarily get the winning shot right away. But the volley can help you construct the winning shot.

The best way to construct a winning shot is by volleying the ball to your opponents' weakest shot. The weakest shot is usually the low backhand shot of your opponent.

One rule of thumb goes like this: a good low-shot is always good, and a bad high shot is always bad. I picked up this lesson from two great coaches, Coach Mo and Coach Matty. During the volley shots, you generally want to keep the ball low. It's better to use those odds to your advantage.

Types of Volley Shots

Here are a few descriptions of the types of volley shots:

- *DEEP VOLLEY*—Hitting the ball deep toward your opponents' base-line because your opponent is deep. Your target is their feet. When they're deep, keep 'em deep.

Paddle high, 10:00 (am or pm) ☺, volley ready position.

Punch volley straight ahead, paddle face slightly open.

- *KITCHEN VOLLEY (VOLLEY DINK)*—Hitting the ball into your opponents' kitchen area to make them hit up on the ball or for you to reset the rally.
- *VOLLEY LOB*—Hitting the ball up and over the head of your opponent. This volley is mainly used when your opponent is up at the kitchen and you hit the ball into the court behind them. Ideally, it will surprise them, and they won't be able to return the shot effectively. Much like the disguised dink lob, the volley lob is best when disguised.

TRANSITION AREA SHOTS

The transition area is between the baseline and several feet behind the kitchen line (or no man's land). With each ball hit into your court, you need to quickly determine if you will attack or settle. This is an area of the game where practice and applying patience and discernment will develop the precision of your response. Determining to attack or settle the ball depends on where the ball is located in relation to your body: low at your feet, hip level, chest level, or above your shoulders.

Here is a breakdown for determining if a ball should be attacked or settled:

1. If the ball is above your shoulders, attack.
2. If the ball is between your shoulders and your hips, you can choose to attack or settle based on the velocity and position of the ball. If it's near your shoulders and slow, attack. If it's quickly dropping below your waste, settle.
3. If the ball is below your hips (below the net), settle.

Lobbing

The definition of the "lob" shot is not always clear in the minds of many players I've met. Here is a definition:

Lobbing is hitting the ball upwards intending the ball to fly over your opponents' heads and land somewhere in the back third of your opponents' court.

There are two primary situations when lobbing should be used:

1. disguising a lob as a dink when you are at the non-volley line to surprise your opponent by hitting the ball over their head; OR
2. when you are off balance and or out of position to give yourself enough time to recover, by lobbing high and deep and getting back into position

It's important to point out that having an overreliance on lobbing will *not* allow you to improve. You may win rallies, but lobbing by default will limit the development of more important shots and strategies.

Making a lob shot at the wrong time or if it's hit poorly will make you vulnerable since they can be particularly easy to attack. For that reason, I typically avoid relying on the lob except for the first situation, a disguised lob, because if done well, it can be a great surprise shot. However, I also resort to the lob when I am caught off-balance and out of position, as it gives me an opportunity to stay alive and return to a strong position at the kitchen line (non-volley line).

Third Shot

This critical shot occurs after the serve (the first shot) and after the return of serve (the second shot). You've served, your opponent has returned your serve and it is now time for you to hit the third shot. This is the shot that differentiates low level players from advanced players. Your ability to effectively drive or drop the 3rd shot will determine your level of play.

We'll assume that your opponents are smart players and mobile. Therefore, you should expect that 100% of the time your opponents will be at the kitchen line as you begin your third shot. However, during recreational play or low level play, you will find that both players are not always at the kitchen line. In that case, you may adjust the percentage of times you hit a drop versus a drive based on your opponents skill level and mobility. If one of your opponents doesn't come to the kitchen line, hit a drive to keep them back. No reason to hit a drop shot which enables them to get to the kitchen line. Your job is to get to the kitchen line and when possible, prevent them from getting to the kitchen line.

Now, back to playing at a higher level against smart and mobile players. Your choices for a third shot are you can drive a hard shot back at them or hit a drop shot into the kitchen. Both are good strategies. Regardless which shot you select, the objective is to enable you and your partner to get to or at least closer to the kitchen line.

The drive is simply a hard forehand or backhand targeted at your opponents weakest shot, a gap between them and or directed to the person that is moving. The drop shot is a lofty shot that lands in the kitchen, forces your opponent to hit up on the ball and gives you time to get closer to the kitchen line.

The original expert on this shot and whose shot I emulate is my friend, Dave Weinbach. You can see videos of Dave's third shot drop shot on YouTube.

What to do after you've hit your third shot? There are two key elements to what to do after your third shot. First, if you've hit an unattackable ball, move forward towards the kitchen, stopping into your ready position before your opponent hits the ball. Second, if you've hit an attackable ball, do not move forward mindlessly. Instead, stop into your ready position and when your opponent hits the ball back to you, hit a 5th shot drop or drive. If your 5th shot is unattackable, advance as you would on the 3rd shot. If your 5th shot is attackable, hunker down as you would after hitting an attackable 3rd shot. Repeat this process until you hit an unattackable ball and are able to advance to the kitchen line. Please refer to **MY FAVORITE DRILLS** for a great drill to improve the critical third shot.

SPECIAL SHOTS

- **ERNE**—This is an advanced level shot. The Erne shot is used to skirt the rule that prevents you from hitting the ball when stepping into

Put one foot outside the court and straddle the line.

Put both feet out of court and attack the ball soon after it crosses the net.

the kitchen area. You do this by actually stepping outside the court or jumping over the kitchen into the area adjacent to the kitchen. From there, you reach back over your sideline and hit the shot back into your opponents' court. It is not an illegal shot, because you are not in the kitchen when you make the shot. This shot is for advanced level playing, so don't worry if you don't get it immediately.

- **AROUND THE POST**—This is an advanced level shot that is used in high-level play. To make an around the post shot, you step outside your court to retrieve your opponent's wide cross-court shot that bounced in your kitchen and is now wide of the net post. Instead of

Step outside the court and get your paddle down low.

Be patient, ensure the ball is wide of the post and hit it low back into opponent's court around the post.

hitting the ball back over the net directly, you hit the ball around the net post. The purpose is to catch your opponent off guard and hit at a difficult angle for them to return.

MY STUDENTS' FAVORITE LESSONS

The following three sections are a collection of 35 of my student's favorite lessons. They include many anecdotes and sayings to make it easier for you to remember what you learn. In writing them down here, I hope to give you a taste of what it's like to have some great moments of personal coaching. You may find these lessons to be the most valuable part of the book.

Due to the constraints of making a book, I could not include every lesson here. But I have included 35 of the best to be exact, and they will greatly improve your playing. I hope that you will be able to apply these lessons in a way that both improves your game and is fun along the way!

I use some phrases and colloquialisms to describe these lessons to make them more memorable on the court. I want them to stay in my student's minds longer. These lessons in the following sections are designed to be concise, insightful nuggets that have been tested over the years and will absolutely help you improve your game when applied on the court correctly.

Introductory Lesson: Enough About the History and Rules, Let's Play!
The vast majority of my students don't need, or want, to hear some long dissertation about the rules and history of pickleball. That's why we immediately focus on playing the game at the start of the first lesson. We begin hitting balls immediately after discussing our objectives for the lesson. Simply hitting the shots and moving around the court, will be how you will put these lessons into practice. You will learn the game quickly when you apply

these principles in a way that works for your present skill level and physical condition.

Remember this introductory lesson, because sometimes I meet players who come from other instructors, clinics, or playing situations where they feel a bit overwhelmed with too much jargon or lengthy instructions. You will not find that in this book! These special lessons are designed to play the game correctly, not simply talk about it.

PART I: TAKING SHOTS

When I coach people, the first thing they want to learn is how to make good shots. So we'll start out with these lessons on how to prepare for and make good shots.

#1 Just Don't Miss!

On the surface, this idea seems so obvious. I'll break it down to explain what I mean. Don't try for some magical shot when a straightforward shot will do. Don't go for that hard to reach corner shot or a risky baseline shot. Hit the high percentage shots that you are well positioned to take and that don't require excessive movements. Focus your energy on making the shot you can make well, and just don't miss!

This principle actually originated from a close friend of mine, Dick Johnson, who was the best 70-year-old tennis player in the United States. I firmly believe Dick would have been the number one pickleball player for his age in the United States. Unfortunately, he passed away right before the U.S. Open, but his wisdom lives on to benefit many students.

Shortly after Dick passed away, I went with some students to the U.S. Open. They wore shirts that said "Just Don't Miss" in memory of our dear friend and a fabulous player. Follow his wise words, and the game will become a bit easier to play.

Another great thing Dick said was, "Don't hit a dollar shot, when a dime shot will do."

Just do as Dick says. You'll have more fun.

Dick's wise words to play better pickleball.

> **REMEMBER**   Most points in pickleball come from unforced errors, not outright winning shots. Focus on the "just don't miss" principle and your game will improve. I recommend repeating this phrase in your head during drills, practice, open play, and competitive play.

#2 Don't Lose a Rally on a Shot You Can't Win It On

If you're standing in a ready position at the kitchen line (non-volley zone line), and the ball is hit toward you and begins to fall to land below the net, it's very hard to hit a winning shot from that angle. The best option here is just hit the ball back over and get to the next shot. No sense in losing this rally by trying for something lucky or magical.

Using discernment will help you to quickly detect when a ball is falling below the attackable level. When a ball falls below the net it is no longer attackable. You have to settle the ball by hitting it back safely over the net. This makes your play less stressful, as you can focus on attacking the balls that you can and avoid attacking the shots where all you should do is settle.

Just don't lose a rally on a shot that you can't win it on anyway. Be patient, you'll probably get a much better chance to hit a winner or construct the rally on the next shot.

#3 How to Play Against Bangers

Bangers are those people whose main go-to shot seems to always be smashing the ball as hard as they can. It often comes from tennis or racquetball players, or novice players who have yet to learn the game strategy or develop soft hitting skills.

The main hang-up I see with students is there is an intimidation factor that can disrupt their playing. There's no need to be intimidated by bangers. The game is designed to mitigate banger tactics like this, overpowering your opponent by smashing the ball. Also, the game is more fun when rallies last longer.

To handle a banger, follow this process:

1. Get to the kitchen line.
2. Stay calm.
3. Get in and remain in a ready position.
4. Don't try for a magical return shot.
5. Make punch volley shots (short, punching backhand hits with no backswing) to keep them deep in their court, or hit to their feet.
6. Continue until the banger hits it out of bounds or you get an opening for a winning shot.

Correct court position, ready position, and demeanor (calm).

The Bangers wall, bangers eventually bang the ball into the net or long.

Keep in mind, about 30% of the balls will go long if the ball is hit hard and it's above your shoulders, so use discernment.

Basically, what ends up happening is you set up a virtual wall deflecting those banger hits back to them. Don't waste time trying to change the direction of the ball. Just block it back to return the ball.

If your opponent is back deep, hit it back deep. Since they are hitting it hard, they are putting all the pace on the ball, so you won't need to hit it hard to send it back deep.

Continue blocking for as long as you need to. If your opponent continues banging the ball and you've blocked it, typically the second or third smash will go into the net or go long. As in many other cases, it is an unforced error by your opponent that will allow you to win the rally.

#4 The Net Is Like a Lake on a Par 3
Those reading this who've done some golfing are likely already familiar with this concept. In golf, when hitting on a Par 3, you just need to hit the golf ball over the lake onto the green. The net in pickleball works similar to the lake. Remove it from your field of vision. Just hit the ball over the net!

PRO TIP   When the ball is low, you just need to return the ball over the net. There's not much else you can do. Preferably, you can hit your return shot to land at your opponents' feet. If the ball is at your shoulder level, you should attack the ball, and you will win roughly 90% of the time.

The net is 2" higher at the sideline, the ball does not go over.

The net is 2" lower in the middle. Hit the ball over the lake. Oops, I mean the net.

Pickleball is a sport that is best played with a high margin of error. This essentially means to clear the net with plenty of space! There's not much benefit to keeping it close to the net as you hit it over. Just get the ball over the net—that's half the victory.

#5 Create the Gap, See the Gap, Hit the Gap

This lesson is an example of creating opportunities for you to win the rally by constructing the rally. The purpose is getting one or both of your opponents out of position to create a gap or opening that you can hit the ball through.

Here are the steps to creating, seeing and hitting the gap:

1. Start a gap by hitting the ball to one side of your opponents' court to move them in that direction. If they start to turn their body, that is a good sign they'll be late getting back to their correct ready position.
2. If the gap exists after your first shot, go ahead and hit the gap.
3. Widen the gap by hitting the ball to the other side to move the other opponent toward the other edge of the court.
4. See the gap as each opponent moves to a far side of the court. It is likely that your opponent doesn't return to the middle, their partner doesn't cover the middle, and/or one or both of your opponents are off-balance and out of position. As soon as any of these occur, proceed as follows:
5. Hit the ball through the gap.

Setting up this gap may take several shots before it opens up, so patience is useful. Another approach to constructing the point and hitting the gap is to repeatedly hit the ball down the middle, between your opponents. As soon as one of your opponent reaches too far or is out of balance and unable to return to their ready position, hit the ball wide of the person who is off balance. Don't switch to hitting the ball to the person who is in balance and poised in their ready position. Continue hitting to the person who is off-balance, making them reach to return your shot.

I recommend learning this technique early on. It takes some time and patience to perfect.

> **PRO TIP** At advanced playing levels, this is one example of where you could use spin to make your shots harder for your opponent to hit well.

#6 Poaching with a Friend

Pickleball is most often played as doubles. Poaching, or stepping into your teammate's side of the court to hit the ball, is inevitable. The extent to which you poach, if at all, should be determined by your level of competition and prior agreement with your partner. If you are playing competitively, whoever has the best shot, not necessarily the better or stronger player, should always take the shot.

On poaching, one student shared the following:

"I believe poaching can be a powerful weapon if it's for a clear winner, especially if your partner is back. It can be a detriment if you play with someone who poaches because they think they are a better player and take your shots. This causes partner frustration, which can result in unforced errors. Players need to trust their partners."

A common situation is when you are on the left side (odd side) of your court and your teammate is on the right side (even side). The ball comes down the middle, angling toward the right side. For you, it's your forehand, but for your teammate, this would be their backhand. Why don't you just step over and use your forehand to make the stronger shot?

Your teammate's backhand will usually be weaker than your forehand, so the forehand is clearly the better shot.

Step forward and towards your partner to hit a forehand poach.

Sometimes in recreational play or other open play scenarios, you will have players who prefer to hit all the balls that come into their side of the court. That's totally acceptable if that's what you've agreed on. In rec play, it's important to talk with your partner before you start playing and ask, "Would you like me to poach or not to poach?"

If you want to play competitively and win games, poaching is necessary. Effective poaching involves ridding yourself of an unnecessary ego and allowing the person with the best shot to make the shot. Talented opponents will always be using poaching techniques, so it is essential for you to use them, too, when you compete at higher levels.

SUGGESTION: Friendly poaching may be a new concept to some players. If so, remember to have a discussion with your partner before you are playing. Make sure you are both comfortable with poaching and how you intend to play. It may seem rude to take a shot headed toward your partner. But ultimately, the hit should go to who has the best shot, and that may be either partner. You and your partner must agree on the level of play.

#7 Poach to Win, Not to Play

Players need to remember that with poaching, you are poaching to hit winning shots, not just to continue the play with a volley shot. This concept

Intercept the ball, hit a winner or set up the winner.

builds on the "poaching with friends" concept. As you will need to poach to play competitively in doubles, this is a critical technique to get right.

Here's a scenario:

SCENARIO: The ball comes over the net and is going toward your partner's side of the court. You have better positioning or a stronger shot, and you take it. Next, you need to make sure that you make a winning shot to win the rally.

In other words, make sure the shot that you are poaching is attackable and that you can put it away.

You are making a shot to win, not a volley to just hit. You should not poach a shot from your partner and then just hit a returnable shot to your opponent. Your partner can do that just as well as you can.

Poaching is intended for those moments where you have an opening and you can put the shot away for a winner.

#8 Punishing Short Returns

This shot is an important shot to get right. If you do get it right, you will score many points with it. When your opponent makes the mistake of hitting up a short-high return that bounces (above the net), these are the kind of shots that you can easily hit right back for a winning shot. Whenever this happens, your prior third shot strategy should be tossed out the window. Hit the ball back hard using your best groundstroke, and win the point!

This often comes up when you and your teammate have a prepared strategy on how to hit and respond. Inevitably, since most points in pickleball come from unforced errors, there will be a mistake made. Short returns are probably the easiest ones for deciding what to do. Hit it back with 75% power and down the middle for a winner.

When a short high bouncing return is hit up, players sometimes want to hold to their third shot strategy. This is a mistake. If you're given a good opening, just take it!

Make 'em pay by hitting forehand down the middle for winner or to set up the winner.

Also, you should only use about 75% of your strength when hitting this shot. If you hit much harder than 75% of your strength, you will sacrifice control. This also applies to all other types of hits. When you hit above 75% strength on any shot, you lose a lot of your ability to control the shot.

REMEMBER   Most points in pickleball come from unforced errors. That is what you are setting up in this shot. Your opponent makes a mistake in their shot, and you take full advantage of that opportunity. Short high returns are a great opportunity to get an easy point if you see it early, toss out your plans, hit the right shot, and get the point.

#9 Hit the Angle, Please Don't Hit the Angle

Because it is hard to see and predict where the ball will end up there is no hard and fast rule on whether or not you should hit certain angles. Use your discernment, make your best judgment, and exercise patience to wait for the right ball, rather than try and force a winning shot too early in the rally.

My two guiding elements to hitting the angle shot are:

1. When the ball is in front of you and above your shoulders, you have a good position to hit down on it, so hit down. That is one angle. The other angle, assuming you're hitting downward, is to hit toward a sideline.
2. When the ball is losing momentum and falling below your waist, don't hit it down. It will go into the net. Instead make a safe shot and wait for a better opportunity to hit a winner.

This takes some time to read the small differences in the angle and position of the ball. The earlier you can spot these changes, the better.

Above shoulder, in front of body, hit down and hit angle.

Callahan Pickleball Academy classes in action

Callahan Pickleball Academy students won medals in tournaments

Callahan Pickleball Academy students at pickleball parties

PART II: MOVEMENT AND POSITIONING

#10 Running While Hitting Violation

Notice the tape measure, stop early to avoid hitting while running.

One of the most important habits to develop is to stop moving as soon as your opponent begins a backswing.

This is a difficult skill for many players. The best place to win rallies is from the kitchen line, and players are understandably anxious to get as close as they can to the kitchen. Sometimes players keep running toward the kitchen without any regard to how soon they are going to be hitting the ball.

Getting to the kitchen line is important, but it is more important to be in a ready position before you hit the ball. Remember, your readiness and court position is more important than your speed.

Running (and also moving or repositioning) while hitting will cause you to lose some of your balance. Losing even a little balance will usually mess up your return shot. It is only about five to seven steps from the baseline to the kitchen. Keep an eye on your opponent, and as soon as your opponent begins to wind up for a return, stop where you are and get into a well-balanced ready position. After you've returned the shot, you can calmly advance the remaining few steps to the kitchen line.

Many players don't even realize how running while hitting interferes with their shot. My student Carolyn shared this:

"I learned this from repetitive lessons that pointed out why I had hit the ball into the net, because you're running through the ball. It was constantly pointed out to me. So the more I did it, the more I learned where I was making a mistake and started to avoid doing it."

In pickleball, the best players learn to watch their opponents from a distance and stop moving as soon as they see their opponent start a backswing. After you have stopped, the next step is to get into your ready position. Once you make your return hit, you can start moving again until you see your opponent start to make another backswing.

My student Charlie shared this:

"The number one thing I learned from your classes is to watch your opponent's hand, paddle, and ball and track them all the way and stop early."

In summary, it's not easy to change your movement habits. As I've seen, many players just keep moving because they're so anxious to get to the kitchen line. Good players learn to get in the habit of stopping early and settling into a ready position long before their opponent connects with the ball. That way, you'll be set up to make a good shot!

#11 Minimalist Movement

The "minimalist movement" principle applies to all movements that you'll make on the court. The lesson is exactly what it sounds like. Only make movements that are necessary to move forward and be prepared to hit the ball. This applies to both your body movement and paddle movements.

In particular, pay attention to these three body movements:

1. Minimize follow through swings.
2. Minimize shoulder turns and cross steps.
3. Minimize backswings beyond what is necessary.

For your paddle, the goal is to keep the paddle face toward the target through the impact zone for the longest period possible. You shouldn't be flipping it back and forth unnecessarily before, during and after the shot.

#12 Who Wants to Run?

Some reading this may remember the renowned UCLA basketball Coach John Wooden once said, "Be fast, but don't hurry."

I love this quote. It expresses the benefit of moving fast while avoiding the kind of mindless running that can easily wear you out or put you off balance when hitting a shot. Why run when you can hit a strategic shot that will allow you to walk up to the kitchen line?

Here is a scenario to demonstrate: You serve to me. I hit the ball hard back to you.

This means I will have to run up to the kitchen line to get there before you hit the third shot. Why do I want to run?

Try this instead: Hit a lofty deep return. (Thank you, Sarah Ansboury.)

This gives you the time to walk up (or perhaps briskly jog) to the kitchen after you have hit it.

Hitting that lofty deep return will avoid excessive running and also allow you to be more prepared for whatever your opponent hits back at you.

Good strategic shots can allow you to avoid running like a chicken with your head cut off. Balance and preparation are more important than overall speed.

Who wants to run when, by playing smarter you don't have to?

> **PRO TIP**   On a service return, you must decide whether to give your opponent more or less time to return the ball. You can either hit a hard and low forehand or a loftier return to afford you more time to get into the kitchen. Try counting the number of seconds it takes once the ball leaves your paddle to when it bounces. The difference from a hard low shot and lofty shot landing is about 1.5–3.0 seconds. A lofty return shot will give you about double the time to cover the seven steps to get to the kitchen.

#13 Your Ready Position is Determined by Your Court Location

Here are three ready positions to use for different court locations:

1. **Baseline Position**—When standing at the baseline position, the stance is similar to a tennis stance. Your paddle is pointed directly in front of you, toward noon.

Knees bent, face opponent hitting the ball, paddle ready.

2. **Transition Area**—Stop, squat, paddle down in front of and below your knees, weight forward, open paddle face so that the ball goes over the net without you swinging the paddle.

Ready to defend, hit and approach the NVL.

Go Blues, defend the goal, defend the transition area.

Learn from the 2019 Stanley Cup Champion, St. Louis Blues.

It might be helpful to envision how a hockey goalie is positioned. When faced with opponents, he keeps his hockey stick on the ice ready and blocking off access to the goal. Raise your paddle slightly off the ground. For the kitchen position, raise the paddle in front of your chest.

Paddle up, 10:00, in front of your chest, but not so far you over-reach.

3. **Kitchen Position**—When standing at the kitchen, it's best to assume that most volleys are going to fly to your backhand. So, you want to stand with your paddle pointed at somewhere between 9 o'clock and 10 o'clock. You want the paddle held up somewhere in front of your chest. That's the ready position for the kitchen.

> **PRO TIP**   Always be moving up to get within an inch of the kitchen line and remain there. The only real exception to this is if you hit a lob that doesn't go over your opponent by accident. Your opponent may be able to smash that lob right back at you. To avoid getting hit in your face, you need to safely back up a few feet.

#14 3rd Shot Partner Advance
This is a technique that you can use all the time when you're playing doubles.

Get 3 steps closer to NVL, go or stay depends on shot.

Here's how it works:

Your opponent hit a serve return toward your partner. You can see the angle and direction of this shot from 44 to 48 feet away. When you see this, take three steps forward, and then briefly glance backward to make sure your partner is making a solid shot.

REMINDER   You don't always want to rush ahead. Generally speaking, you do want to stay parallel with your partner. This is one of those exceptions where it's okay to be out of sync and move up first, assuming your partner can get to the kitchen line quickly, and/or you both decide to stay back to return an attackable ball hit to your opponent.

After you make sure your partner makes a good shot, what reason do you have to stay back? Use this precious time to your advantage by moving toward the kitchen! If you move up these three steps, you would already be almost half the way to the kitchen!

#15 Be Balanced Before, During, and After the Shot

Most people understand the basic idea that balance is good. But what I see that is often overlooked is maintaining your balance before, during, and after the shot. Making the shot can temporarily throw off your balance, so it's helpful to develop the habit of paying attention to your balance at these points of a shot.

To give some context to this, many people tell me they want "good form." That's great. However, it's impossible to have good form when you're out of balance. For good form, balance is the place to start. If you have a good balance it is *likely* that good form will follow.

Balanced before, correct ready position, weight slightly forward.

Balanced during, calm weight transfer towards target, feet underneath.

Balanced after, be careful of excessive follow-through like this.

To improve your balance for your shot, monitor your balance at each stage:

1. In your ready position before you hit the ball
2. As you take a step to hit the ball
3. After you hit the ball

If you're out of balance at one of these steps you're doing something wrong. Maybe you're hitting the ball too far in front of you. Maybe you have excessive follow-through. Maybe your footwork is off. Look for ways to improve your balance.

#16 Just Say "Good Shot" and Don't Run Backward

This is a cautionary lesson to help you avoid one of the most common injuries in pickleball.

Picture this scenario:

You hit the ball toward your opponent. Then your opponent hits a lob that flies well over your head to land in the court well behind you. If you start backing up quickly you can easily get tripped up on your feet and risk getting seriously injured.

This can happen to the best of players. It's avoidable and unnecessary. Instead of backing up, just say nice shot, and get on with it. Pick your battles and avoid a low percentage shot that could risk getting yourself hurt.

If you decide to try to run down the lob, turn away from the net, move forward to your baseline, plant your back foot, return the shot, and move toward the kitchen. Don't back up!

PART III: DISCERNMENT, PATIENCE, AND WISDOM

Anyone who has spent time playing pickleball has likely observed that there is no shortage of self-appointed "pickleball experts" on the courts. These people sometimes offer an abundance of unsolicited playing advice. This may or may not be helpful. My students have learned that the best response to this situation is to simply say, "I have a coach. Today, I'm just here to have fun."

I do believe that, most of the time, people have good intentions. But even if people give worthwhile advice, it may not be right for you at your stage of development. Players need the right advice at the right time. Self-appointed experts on the courts are usually not in the best position to judge your playing needs, level of play, or provide coaching.

Should this situation arise, I recommend just saying, "I have a coach. Today, I'm just here to have fun." This ensures you still enjoy playing and avoid the hassle of someone scrutinizing and picking apart your every move.

REMINDER   Recall from the lesson "Enough About the History and Rules, Let's Play!" that it is important to have fun while making progress. If you encounter a "pickleball expert," just shrug it off and keep playing. Don't obsess over techniques when you're out doing rec play. Having fun, making friends, and getting some good exercise should be your goals.

#17 Practice the Art of Discernment

In my coaching, I frequently reference the importance of using discernment. What do I mean by discernment? I mean the ability to judge, adjust on the fly, and make the best shot selection.

One student shared that what helped her the most in better using discernment was "understanding that you have time to relax and hit the right shot."

Your opponents' position and movement, their swings, the velocity and elevation of the ball, your own position, your partner's position, how and where you should hit the ball are some examples of what to discern. Combine all of this with other environmental factors, such as wind or other players, and there can easily be a lot of noise. Therefore, you need to be able to easily pick out and focus on what is important.

Developing your discernment involves two elements:

A) knowing what to look for; and

B) understanding your shot selection options.

Discernment involves all aspects of the game. The most common use of discernment is judging whether you should attack or settle a ball. As discussed earlier, there are times to attack, and there are times to settle. The more quickly and intuitively you can make this determination in the heat of the moment, the better your game will be.

My student Carolyn said this about improving her discernment over time:

"It came from observing other people try shots that wouldn't work. And seeing people try shots over and over again that didn't work validated the guidance I was getting on which shots to avoid."

REFRESHER   Here's a simple breakdown to remember. If above your shoulders, attack. If below the net, settle. If in between, use discernment to decide whether to attack or settle.

#18 I Just Want to Look Good

I want my students to play well, but I also want them to look good while playing.

Looking good requires a foundation of skills, early preparation, muscle memory, experience, and the use of discernment to apply the lessons. This will enable you to handle the various scenarios that will be thrown at you!

Consider these six points:

- You can only look good if you have proper form.
- You can only look good if you are in a ready position when the ball comes.
- You can only look good if you have good balance.
- You can only look good if you are in the right position on the court.
- You can only look good if you are hitting the right shots.
- You can only look good if you are calm.

Looking good is a worthwhile objective. These six points above are essential to getting there the right way. Follow those six points and the other advice in this book, and you will certainly look good playing.

#19 Playing Consistent Pickleball vs. Hero/Zero Pickleball

One student shared this about playing consistent pickleball:

"It is amazing to watch students evolve into relaxed, consistent players. Hard slamming transforms into relaxed drop shots from all areas of the court. This has been the biggest game changer for me, and allows me to enjoy the game so much more."

Think about those moments of play in pickleball when you find yourself off balance. Think about when you lose your position or are otherwise unable to make a good shot. Does it make sense to try to make a winning shot (a hero shot) from a bad position?

In these situations, use your discernment to sense how what looks and feels like a bad shot will really be a bad shot (a zero shot). Avoid making these low percentage shots. Consistent play should be your goal. Don't seek out making the extraordinary hero/zero shots.

For instance, when you're off balance and out of position, I generally recommend hitting up a lob as a recovery shot. Put the lob up high in the deep center of your opponent's court. This will give you enough time to regain your balance and get in a better position.

My student Charlie made a great point about taking multiple high percentage shots:

> *"The best players will vary their shots. Long shots, short shots, soft shots, and hard shots. If every shot is the same, it's obvious a player is not improving or will be easy to play against. Using multiple high percentage shots is the key to improving."*

Overall, it is far better to be in the habit of taking the high percentage shots. Your consistency and game will improve. You will also excel at the basics, which is where the game is most often won or lost.

#20 Numbers Don't Lie, Play the Statistics to Win

Building on the concept of playing a high percentage game, here are a few stats to consider:

- The first team to the kitchen wins almost 90% of the time! This is why you should always be moving toward the kitchen. It's just seven steps away!
- About 30% of the hard balls hit to you while you're in the kitchen will be out of bounds.
- A high percentage of misses at the kitchen line are swinging volleys.

Punch volley: extend the paddle versus swing the paddle.

Why are there so many kitchen volley misses? Players often take a tennis-style windup by making a big backswing. This causes the face of your paddle to point outward in all different directions. This makes the ball's trajectory and direction vary based on when it's hit, which is not good for playing high percentage pickleball. It can also cause late hits, sending the ball out of bounds instead of down the middle.

The solution to this is to use a "punch" volley to hit the ball. You just need to extend your arm and the paddle forward enough to hit the ball firmly. This saves time and energy, and it improves your control of the ball all at the same time!

In summary, get to the kitchen first, don't over swing, and you will be playing much better.

> **REMEMBER**   As discussed before, only use minimal movements. Avoid unnecessary windups and excessive follow-through on your swings whenever possible.

#21 Low Percentage Shots to Avoid

This lesson builds on the last lesson about playing consistently and taking high percentage shots. Here are a few examples of the kinds of "low percentage" shots I mentioned that you really should avoid altogether:

1. Hitting the ball hard when it's below the net.
2. Hitting the ball hard when it's at the net height.
3. Hitting the ball as hard as you can.
4. Hitting the ball into the kitchen when the opponent is back at the baseline.

When an opponent is back, you want to keep them back. The more you keep your opponent back, the worse their shots will get, and the better your chances for winning the rally will be.

You will find exceptions to these rules, but students who follow these guidelines will avoid making many of those low percentage shots on the court.

#22 Give Them the Sideline, They'll Miss Anyway (Playing the Statistics)

One in, one out, a high percentage of balls hit to just a few inches inside the sideline go out. Let 'em try.

Here is another method you should practice to play the odds in your favor. During your defense, focus on covering the middle areas of the court. When it comes to the sideline shots, don't spread yourself too thin by trying to cover the sideline.

Covering the sideline shots is not worth the physical energy or the mental effort. Those sideline shots often miss. In pickleball, you're better off aiming for the middle to avoid aiming too close to the sidelines. Statistically, you will perform much better because you'll hit far less balls out of bounds. Let your opponents go for the sidelines. The closer they aim for the sideline, the more they hit out of bounds.

#23 They Only Played Pickleball Twice. Why Are They So Good?

You may notice how some players start playing and they pick up the sport right away. In most of these instances, these are players with years of tennis or other racquet/paddle sports. The important thing is not to get thrown off by somebody's quick learning curve or ability to hit some good shots immediately.

My student Carolyn had this to say about this topic:

"At the tennis club where I played, there was a group of tennis players that came to a pickleball class. They were good right away. Here I was, taking lots of pickleball classes and I still wasn't as good as they were. It's because they had already hit a million forehands. But, I continued to work hard and now I'm able to use my soft game to counter their hard game."

The reality is that until you get into playing up against the kitchen and other strategic aspects of pickleball, many moves are similar to tennis. A forehand in pickleball looks a lot like a forehand in tennis.

> **REMEMBER**   90% of tennis skills are transferable, such as coordination, footwork, and weight transfer, so it shouldn't be a big surprise that some tennis players pick up the sport quite quickly.

You will sometimes see players who've been hitting tennis forehands for a lifetime make flawless pickleball forehands. That's fine, you can still play well against them. Additionally, pickleball is one of the few sports that was specifically designed to minimize any physical advantages. Strategy, with a good dose of discernment and patience, can go a long way toward mitigating any advantages that good players from other sports might possess.

#24 Hit Through the Ball, Not at It

This is a lesson in hitting the ball well by extending the impact zone. When you hit the ball, your swing should not stop immediately when it hits the ball. Your swing should not wrap around your body either. You should hit the ball with enough follow-through to hit three balls if they were stacked right behind each other.

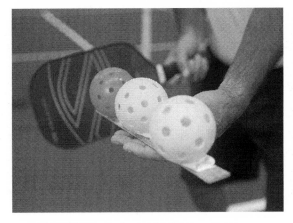

Imagine hitting three balls in a row, paddle stays in impact zone longer.

Paddle stays in impact zone longer, you'll hit balls more solid.

You should be able to feel a good hit through your wrist and hand. If the ball is hit well-centered on your paddle and you have the right force, you will know you hit the sweet spot. This will maximize the effectiveness of your shot while minimizing the movement and power required.

It will take some time and practice to build up the right feel.

REMEMBER   As discussed before, you always want to eliminate unnecessary movements, so remember not to overswing. It's best to accelerate your movement as you make a connection with the ball.

#25 Partner Talk

Talking with your partner during a rally should be specific and minimal. Here are some code words to keep player communication quick during the game.

> You (or yours)—your partner's shot
> Me (or I)—your shot
> Out—when you think the ball will go out of bounds
> Bounce—when the ball may be out and you want your partner to let it bounce
> Back—stay back or back off the non-volley zone (kitchen)
> Go—move toward the non-volley zone (kitchen)

#26 Talk and Don't Talk to Your Partner

> **REMEMBER**   Keep all talk positive. Complimenting good moves fosters a much better atmosphere than criticizing each mistake.

I have more to say about the topic of talking while playing. Most of the time, pickleball is a doubles game. When you're playing, you need to coordinate shots and movements. These are the times when you should talk to your partner.

Excessive talking, "coaching" and criticizing can be a hard habit for some players to break. Over time, you will learn to develop a comfortable and encouraging form of communication that works for you.

> **FUN TIP**   Of course, if you're just enjoying a relaxed game with friends, have fun and talk away. When you're having a great time, talking is strongly encouraged!

#27 Watch and Don't Watch Your Partner

This simple lesson builds on the lesson **3rd Shot Partner Advance**. When you are at the baseline with your partner awaiting the 3rd shot, watch your partner if the ball comes back to him or her. Once you know your partner has made a good shot, a shot that is not attackable, from wherever you are, you can go ahead and move up to the kitchen.

Once you know the shot your partner is making, you have to trust that your partner will make a good shot. Once they've actually made a good shot, watch the ball, not your partner!

Turn to see your partner's shot, advance or stay based on their shot.

> **HINT** Tell your partner your 3rd shot strategy or service return strategy before each serve.

#28 From 44 to 48 feet Away, You See It Coming to Your Forehand

From baseline to baseline, the distance is 44 to 48 feet, depending on the angle. You can train yourself to observe the shot from 44 feet away and know whether it's heading toward your forehand or your backhand. Most people

Starting your backswing when the ball bounces is too late ...

... instead, start your backswing as soon as you see the ball coming to your forehand.

wait for the ball to bounce in their court before they start their backswing. But you don't need to wait if you see it coming from 44 feet away!

If you wait until it bounces, it will be about 5 to 7 feet in front of you. This won't give you enough time to calmly prepare to hit the shot. The sooner you can be ready, and the sooner your paddle is back, the better.

> **PRO TIP**   It takes some discernment in knowing what to look for. One method I use to train students is to have them yell out "forehand!" or "backhand!" as soon as the ball leaves their opponent's paddle. With practice, you can improve your ability to anticipate whether the ball is hit to your forehand or backhand, as well as long or short. This eliminates some of the last second confusion that can occur when hitting the ball.

#29 Cover the Middle, Give them the Pizza Slice

In doubles, you get into this situation all the time. This lesson boils down to making it a priority to cover your most vulnerable areas.

The following scenario will illustrate this point:

You are playing doubles, and all four of you are in the kitchen. Your partner is sent wide to one side as they move to cover a ball. As this happens, the player who was not sent wide needs to move over to cover the middle. By moving over, this will open up the pizza slice, which requires a cross-court shot into the open kitchen area.

The reasons why it's okay to give up this shot are:

A) it's hard to hit; and
B) if they do hit it, it will take more time for the ball to get there, so you will have more time to retrieve the shot.

Therefore, it's really the shot down the middle that we need to cover. If that shot down the middle is hit a bit hard, you will never get there in time to hit it, unless you're already covering the middle.

Perfect positioning to cover the middle.

When your partner moves to the left, you move to the left to cover the middle.

When your partner moves to the right, you move to
the right to cover the middle.

#30 The Game Is More Fun When Rallies Last Longer

Playing longer rallies is more fun. We are all playing pickleball, no matter
our skill level, because it's fun to play. Having longer points will be more sat-
isfying. Here are several shots that cause rallies to end early:

1. The serve is out.
2. The return is too low and hits into the net or too high and it goes out
   of bounds.
3. The third shot is hit into the net or out of bounds.

Each of these is an unforced error that can end a rally in the first three
shots. I recommend trying some of the drills in the section of "My Favorite
Drills" to see how you can improve in these areas.

Also, resist putting spin on the ball as it shortens rallies. Accuracy is low,
and the dynamics with the ball, paddle, and the court are just not conducive
to hitting spin shots until you get to a very high level of playing pickleball.

#31 It's Not "Fire, Ready, Aim"

Those reading this with some military background may be familiar with this phrase, "It's not fire, ready, aim." Ideally, you would never want to hit the ball first and then think about where to hit it later. Get ready, take your aim, and then make your shot. That's the high percentage approach to making shots.

This is something I notice that can be particularly difficult for newer students. They start their forward motion, make their backswing, and hit the ball while still thinking about which shot to make. Make your shot selection, pick your target, and hit the ball last.

#32 Close Your Eyes and Feel the Shot

I have seen many players, who get so excited when they make a shot, look up just before they make contact because they cannot wait to see where the ball goes. More often than not, this will mess up your shot. To get students out of this habit, I have found closing your eyes useful to get a better feel for the shot.

What I do is that I ask students to close their eyes while playing at the kitchen line. We start by dinking shots back and forth. Then I ask students to watch the ball and start their shot. Just before the ball gets to their paddle, they close their eyes.

It makes it easier for students to feel if they hit the ball in the sweet spot or on the edge or tip of the paddle. This is a very important skill and relates to what I mentioned earlier in the book regarding keeping your eyes down and not looking up when you hit the shot. The reason is that looking up to see if it's a good shot will often throw off your shot. Small changes make a big difference.

Building up this sense of knowing if you made a good shot just by feeling it takes time. I recommend practicing this regularly early on to build up sensitivity to the shot. Be patient though. It won't come all at once. Controlling your eyes and monitoring how this affects your shots and body movement is one of those key features that separates novice players from more advanced players.

#33 You Never Looked at the Target, You Never Looked at the Ball

This lesson applies to hitting the serve.

First, you need to look where you are serving to align your mind, body, and your eyes to where you are hitting. Where should you be serving? You should serve to the middle-deep area of the service box (your opponents' court). Sometimes, I see players look at the service area, toss the ball up, and hit it, without ever looking at the ball.

Look at the target, look at the ball, then gently toss or drop the ball, and hit it to the target area. Look at the target, and then look at the ball. A lot of people do one but not the other, or they do them in the wrong order.

A common technique I use to get students to develop a good habit for this process is standing right in front of the students and telling them where their eyes are looking. I say aloud, "You are not looking at the target," or, "You have not looked at the ball," and then, "Look at the target, look at the ball, toss, and hit the ball."

Always look at the ball before you start your service motion. Otherwise, this can happen.

For most people, this is one of those "ah-ha!" moments. Students suddenly realize that they never thought to look at the target and then the ball, but it makes perfect sense. Refer to **Welcome to Your "Happy Serve"** on page 38

#34 It Looked Appetizing, But Now It's Rotten

The scenario for this lesson happens often when players are at the kitchen line.

Here's how it plays out:

1. Your opponent hits up a lofty shot high in the air, you see from across the net that it is above your shoulders, that it looks ready for you to attack and hit a winning shot. It looks appetizing.
2. But by the time the ball gets close enough for you to hit, the ball has dropped so low, below your waist, that you're no longer able to attack it. What was appetizing, is now rotten.
3. At that point, your best option is just to settle it back. Don't try to attack it like you thought you could.

Just like nobody wants to eat rotten food, nobody wants to attack a ball that they should settle!

#35 Don't Put Me in A Pickleball Box

This saying applies to some coaching techniques that I have seen. I absolutely love teaching students that come from tennis or other sports background because so many of their skills are transferable. I really don't think it's wise to tell students to give up any skills they already have.

For example, if you have a good forehand, keep your forehand. I think especially at the baseline it's best to leverage the skills you already have. Your time and energy should focus on harnessing those skills in the right way to maximize your immediate enjoyment of the game and then adapt them to pickleball strategy.

My experience has shown me that students do best with this kind of approach because they don't have to unlearn the skills they already have and their immediate experiences are positive and encouraging. Get yourself having fun, hitting high percentage shots, and being in the right position. You can always tweak your shots and strategies later once you've started to really enjoy the game and have a desire to improve.

10 DANGEROUS MYTHS THAT WILL HURT YOUR GAME

"Deciding what not to do is as important as deciding what to do."
—STEVE JOBS

There are some myths that can really hurt your game. Knowing what not to do can be just as valuable as knowing what to do. These myths cause problems and impede the growth of students all the time.

I have discovered the sources of many of them. Sometimes, they come from other misinformed players. Sometimes, players take something from another sport and erroneously misapply it to pickleball.

Hopefully, we can make some progress in eliminating these myths!

1. Run Faster

I am not sure where this particular myth originated. But many students think that running faster will make them play better. As I've discussed before, your speed is less important than your court position and ready position. Remember, pickleball courts are smaller than tennis courts.

Also, the ball moves a bit slower than most racquet sports. You move around a lot in pickleball, but running fast is not essential. You are better off hitting a strategic shot that enables you to move in while maintaining balance and being ready for the next shot than just hitting the ball hard and running fast. You will move less and be ready when the ball comes back to you.

Now, I am not saying that players are necessarily better off moving slow. You should get to where you are going without delay. But I am saying that just speeding up your movements will not improve your play. Improving your positioning, balance, and readiness will improve your play.

Sometimes, you just need to pay more attention to your movements and court position. Smooth out your technique, stop earlier, and get into your ready position sooner. By discovering these small nuances, you will make big improvements!

2. Get to the Kitchen (Non-Volley Zone) No Matter What!

This myth runs (*pun intended!*) hand-in-hand with the myth "run faster." Some people think that just getting to the kitchen is all that matters. Not true!

Advancing versus running, stopping early to be ready for opponents' shot.

Advancing further in control, in balance and in ready position.

Continuing to advance in control, in balance and in ready position.

You're at the kitchen in balance, in ready position and calm.

You should never sacrifice your readiness just to get to the kitchen. Even though the distance is only 15 feet from baseline to the kitchen, you need to maintain proper balance and be in your ready position to be set up for a good return shot.

3. Hit Your Serve Hard

This myth may come from other sports like tennis where the objective is to overpower your opponent with a hard serve. But if someone is telling you to always just hit the serve or return hard, it means they don't understand the fundamental rules and strategy of pickleball.

Consider this scenario: While serving, you hit the ball hard to me. But what you really did is give me all the pace on the ball to send it back to you.

In other words, you will make it easy for me to hit my return shot because you've done half the work for me. The ball is moving at a fast pace, and it's easy for me to hit it back to you.

But if you hit the serve to me with less pace on the ball, I have to be the one who puts pace on the ball. If I have to put pace on the ball, I am more likely to make a mistake, or hit a weak return.

4. Hit Your Return of Serve Hard

The same dynamics as in "Serve Hard" are at play when you hit a hard return or soft return. Additionally, a lofty return takes around three seconds from paddle to bouncing on the server's side. A hard return takes around a second and a half.

Remember that being in the appropriate ready position for your court position is more important than speed. You want to hit a return shot that gives you enough time to be ready at the kitchen line. Depending on your position on the court, a second and a half may not be enough time for you to get to the kitchen. But the three seconds you get from a lofty return will be enough time! And because of your improved court position, balance and ready position you'll put more pressure on your opponents' third shot.

5. Hit the Ball as Close to the Top of the Net as You Can

This is a common myth that people hear all the time. However, putting the ball close to the net will hurt your game.

Here's why:

1. It increases the unforced errors, causing you to lose more rallies.
2. It gives you less time to move up toward the kitchen.
3. It decreases the length of the points, which is less fun

Pickleball is a sport where you want to give yourself some space and margin for error between the net, sidelines, and baselines.

This shot doesn't clear the net, rally is over.

This shot barely clears the net. Give yourself a bigger margin for error.

I tell students from a golfing background that the net is like a lake on a Par 3 (see page 59). You just get it over. Remove the net from your vision!

REMEMBER   This touches on three earlier lessons: just don't miss, play high percentage pickleball, and just get the ball over the net!

---

6. Always Stay Behind the Line Until the Third Shot is Hit

This lesson applies to playing doubles. This myth involves the following: a player, or his or her partner, will serve, wait for the return of the serve, and then wait for that third shot to be hit before starting to move up. It usually doesn't work as well as coming in a few steps.

Remember that you can see where the ball is going to land from 44 feet away. You can at least easily see that the ball is coming to you or to your partner. Why wait back at the baseline if you already know that your partner, not you, is going to be hitting the third shot? There's no real benefit to waiting. Instead, start moving up in the court once you know the ball is not coming to you. Take two or three steps in, watch your partner's shot, and if it's attackable, you stay back. If the third shot is not attackable, move forward.

Why wait behind the line? Move in, watch your partner, then stay or advance.

> **REMEMBER**   The objective is to be moving toward the kitchen line. This advice dovetails nicely with lesson #14, **3rd Shot Partner Advance**.

7. Put More Spin on the Ball

Only at very high levels of pickleball playing are there some instances to put spin on the ball. For that reason, I recommend avoiding it altogether until you reach those higher levels of play. Make the game easier to play, not harder. Make your shots more consistent, not less. Make rallies last longer, and have more fun.

8. Don't Take a Backswing

Not sure about the origin of this myth, but I work with players that hear it all the time.

I had a student who had an experience with this myth during rec play. While taking her shot from the baseline, she used some backswing to put more force in her forehand shot. In response to this, a well-intentioned player "coach" advised her to not take any backswing. This was wrong because she needed that backswing to hit her forehand shots over the net and deep into the opponents' court.

When you're at the baseline, you are 44 feet away from your opponents' baseline. Most players will need a backswing to make a good deep forehand shot!

> **REMEMBER**   You may recall that we discussed earlier to avoid unnecessary backswings, unnecessary follow-throughs, and other movements. But this doesn't mean that you should eliminate them completely.

9. Just Hit It Hard or Just Hit It Soft

Some pickleball players say you need to just hit hard, while others say you just need to hit soft. Both are wrong!

Some pickleball players get it into their heads that they must either hit it hard or hit it soft. You need to be able to hit both hard and hit soft if you want to have fun and improve at your game. I train students in discernment and shot selection to know how to use both. The appropriate shot depends on your abilities and the specifics of each situation. Mix up your third shots. Hit some as drop shots, and hit some hard. The actual percentage of each is up to you.

10. Go for the Lines

This myth may come from other racquet sports, like tennis, where aiming for the lines is a real benefit at times. But this is not the case in pickleball.

By inches, one is in, one is out. Give yourself a bigger margin for error.

Hitting for the lines are low percentage shots. If you are off by a few inches, you lose the rally. Only at the highest level can players consistently hit the ball within an inch or two of where they intend to hit it.

Why not set your target about two or three feet to the inside of the lines and then construct the rally from there? Reduce unforced errors by not trying to hit one inch inside the lines. You'll have more fun and win more rallies by avoiding the lines.

Hit the ball to your opponents' backhand or forehand, depending on their position and other situational factors. Eventually, you will make shots to your opponent that they will return with weak shots. Plus the returns they make to you will be higher percentage shots for you. This will put you in a position to make a winning shot.

MY FAVORITE DRILLS

"If you don't practice, you don't deserve to win."
—ANDRE AGASSI[3]

Drills are probably not the most exciting part of the game, but they are essential to improving your game and can be surprisingly fun and rewarding. I have seen many students discover some small fault in their playing through a drill. And once they grasp what they were doing wrong, it's as if everything clicks into place.

All these drills have been tested over time and are practical methods to improve your playing. Many of them can be done with just a single partner or coach.

Generally, to get the most out of a drill, I recommend they be done for about 10 to 20 minutes at a time. This gives sufficient time for muscle memory and improved flexibility to kick in. It will also help to identify the specific areas in your playing where you need to improve the most and pick the corresponding drills to sharpen that skill.

As with all my coaching instructions, I always personalize the selection of drills based on my students' needs and present condition. To do this, you should always know your purpose for playing each time you play.

---

[3]Former world tennis champion Andre Agassi played a game of pickleball for the first time in 2018. You can see it here: https://blog.margaritaville.com/2018/04/paddle-battle/

Here are some examples of purpose in playing:

- Are you playing to develop a particular skill?
- Are you going out to play just to meet new people or make some friends?
- Are you just aiming for a good cardio exercise?

TIP 1   For most drills, you want to designate a "feeder." A "feeder" is a coach or friend that throws or hits the ball to the other, allowing them to work on the shot with little pressure. The feeder's job is to make it easy for the partner to work on a desired shot. The feeder should not be trying to make it difficult for the partner to execute the drill correctly or efficiently.

HITTING DRILLS

Banger's Wall

A "banger" is a slang term used to describe those players who just hit the ball as hard as they can on almost every shot. This drill is especially useful for newer players because it will build up a good habit of what to do when playing against a "banger." It will also boost your confidence, which is very important and helps maintain the correct ready position when playing against bangers.

Follow these steps:

STEP 1   Establish a presence at the kitchen line, and get into the ready position.

STEP 2   Have a partner (feeder) throw or hit the balls to you, with increasing speed.

STEP 3   Block the shots using your punch backhand volley.

Build your wall with your partner, your bangers' wall.

In my lesson earlier about playing against "bangers," I discussed how when you receive those lightning speed shots, you don't need to make some magical comeback shot. Your objective is to block the shot, hitting it back to your opponents' feet until they mess up. If you can block it back a few times, the "banger" will usually mess up by hitting it long or into the net.

It's called "banger's wall" because as you practice this you will get to the point where you establish a virtual wall. This virtual wall should switch the power dynamic. Instead of the banger feeling amped up from hitting those intimidatingly hard shots, this type of player will get frustrated and you will throw off their whole game plan.

My student Charlie says this is his favorite drill:

"This drill trains you to have a quick reaction and faster response. You also learn that you don't necessarily need to hit the ball back hard to make a good shot."

Just being a banger is never a great strategy. As mentioned earlier, to be a great player, you need to learn to use both hard and soft shots. Similarly, to be a great player, you need to learn how to manage those tough hard shots from bangers and good players, and this is a great drill to develop the skills of discernment, patience, confidence and shot making.

Taped Kitchen

This is a drill that will require some tape, like painter's tape, to get set up. By changing the court dimensions, you can work on your ability to control and aim our shots.

PART 1 Using tape, set up an artificial line two feet behind the kitchen line, and this will be your new baseline.

PART 2 Play pickleball on this mini-sized court, with a focus on keeping the ball within these new tightly enclosed boundaries.

The purpose of this drill is to train yourself to keep your shots low at your opponents' feet. Over time, you will get your shots to drop right at your opponents' feet in front of or just behind the kitchen line. This drill helps you to hit softer, and reduce the number of attackable balls you hit. It also helps you return those hard-to-hit shots at your feet.

Remember the importance of having your shots clear the net with plenty of room. A very common error in this scenario is making the unforced error of hitting the net, so avoid this at all costs! Try to maintain a wide margin when hitting over the net. A nice trajectory clears the net by a foot or more and still lands at or in front of your opponents' feet.

Two Serves

The focus of this drill is simple: hit your serves deep and toward the middle.
Follow these steps:

STEP 1 Hit the first serve deep, as deep as you possibly can hit.

STEP 2 If the first serve lands out, hit it again.

STEP 3 If second serve lands in, then go ahead and play that point.

I really like how this drill helps remove all that fear of hitting the serve long. We only get one chance to make a serve in pickleball, and this can put a lot of pressure on the serve! Sometimes, that pressure gets us into a habit of not making deep serves. Practicing this drill will help break that habit.

Students can pick up on this concept and see improvements in their serve after running this drill a few times. Many students think their serves are great. Sometimes, this is true, but students are often surprised when they see that this is not exactly true (see **Drill Tip** below).

My student Charlie is like a lot of students. He doesn't like doing this drill, but he knows it makes him a better player, so he continues to do it!

"It's a hard drill, but I force myself to do it. It helps me to hit those serves deep. Without this drill, I don't think I would serve as deep as I do. You want your serves to go deep because if they don't, it'll make it easier for your opponents to get to the kitchen."

Drill Tip for Measuring Your Serves

A good way to measure the accuracy of your serves is to see where your serves actually land. Nobody really likes to be measured, and serving is no different, but this will definitely improve your serves!

To measure your serves, have a coach or friend mark with chalk or tape or any kind of marker where each serve lands. Do this for 10 serves, and the results may surprise you. I did this once with a student, and we found that only two of the 10 serves were actually good. A "good" serve is considered to be in the back third and in the middle of the correct service box.

This drill can be a good wake up call. Once students see the reality of their serves, they pay more attention to what they are doing, and their serves show immense improvement.

Two-Returns

This drill emphasizes a similar technique in the **Two Serves** drill. This drill will also help make better long shots from the baseline. But the focus here is on your return shot, not on the serve. Ideally, you want your return shot to land deep, in the back third of the court, and falling somewhere near the middle of the opponents' court.

Try these steps:

STEP 1   The feeder serves the ball to you.
STEP 2   You try to hit the return as deep as you can.
STEP 3   If the ball goes out of bounds, just serve it again.

Practicing this technique will develop a better mindset for your return. It will improve your comfort by understanding how to return shots with more force, the right trajectory, and to a target in the back third of the court. You will better understand your strengths—and your weaknesses. You will also build your shot selection, targeting and muscle memory.

The final goal in improving your deep returns is to get to the point where you don't have to waste much time, or effort, thinking about what return to make. You just make a good service return, and move in behind it. Remember, 100% of the time you should join your partner at the kitchen line or be near the kitchen line before your opponent hits your service return.

Third Shot Drop and Drive

The third shot is one of the most important and fun shots in the game. We do this drill frequently in our clinics and "play with a pro" training sessions. You'll need four people.

Here is how to set up this drill:

Player #1 is at the baseline ready to hit third shot drops and drives.
Player #2 is at the kitchen line nearest the person at the baseline.
Player #3 is opposite player #1 on the opposite kitchen line across the net.
Player #4 is the feeder, throwing balls which simulate a return of serve.
Player #2 faces the player at the baseline and holds their paddle above their head.

Player #3 extends their paddle towards the middle of their court as if they were poaching.

Now that we're all set up, let's begin the drill.

Player #4 throws or hits a ball (resembling a service return) to the person at the baseline.

Player #1 hits a lofting 3rd shot drop over the extended paddle attempting to land the ball over the net and into the kitchen. Player #2 steps out of the court and out of the way. Another ball is thrown and player #1 hits a cross court third shot drive past the outstretched paddle of player #3. Player #2 then steps back in and holds their paddle up, a ball is thrown and player #1 hits another third shot drop. Continue until each person has hit 10 drops and 10 drives. Rotate positions.

My students love this drill and I've seen significant improvements in their third shot drops and third shot drives. Remember, you want to have both the third shot drop and the third shot drive in your game.

Catch and Volley

This is a delicate drill that will require some patience at first. This one is especially useful for calibrating the right amount of strength and touch for volley shots.

STEP 1   Stand at the kitchen line in your ready position.

STEP 2   Have your feeder hit the ball to you.

STEP 3   Instead of hitting the ball back, use your paddle to deflect it up in the air up about a foot to "catch" it.

STEP 4   As the ball hovers in the air, volley it back across the net.

This drill teaches the art of using "touch" when calibrating how much force to use when hitting the ball. Another element in play here is balancing the paddle face upward, to open the face of the paddle, and to hit the ball

Watch the ball, softly catch it with your paddle, bounce it up just one foot.

Watch the ball and catch it with your non-paddle hand (for advanced practice, bounce the ball on your paddle three times and hit it back to your practice partner).

gently. If done at the right angle and level of force, the ball will bounce gently and upward about one foot.

When I first show students this drill, instead of hitting the ball up a foot, they will hit it up three, four, or even five feet in the air! We don't realize how easily our paddle angle can be controlled, so it's great to practice this drill early when learning to play. This drill also teaches you to soften your grip. Without a soft grip, you will not be able to "catch" the ball. Your control and touch will improve a lot with this! At first, just hit the ball up and catch it with your opposite hand. As your skill improves, hit the ball up three times in a row and then hit it back to your drill partner.

Dink: Three by Three

This dink drill will emphasize two crucial pieces for hitting a good dink shot: *where* to hit the dink and *when* to hit the dink.

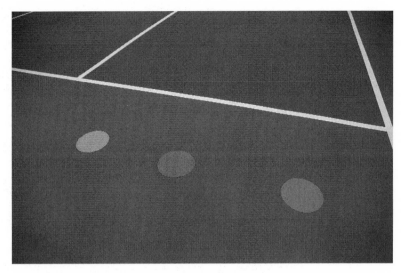

Hit to 3 targets, your opponents' backhand, body and forehand.

First, mark three equal-sized separate circles, horizontally going left to right in the kitchen area with chalk or other targets. The circles roughly represent a third of the court. It also corresponds to your opponents' forehand shot, body shot, and backhand shot.

For the drill, you will be hitting the dink shots into one of these areas. This establishes "where" you will hit the dinks. This works best if you hit to alternate targets. Please, in the drill and in your more competitive games don't hit the same target twice in a row ... move your dinks around by hitting the 3 targets. Hit the first dink to your opponents' forehand, then to their body, and then to their backhand. Each of these shots corresponds, roughly, to one of the three circles drawn on the ground.

The second half of the drill is deciding on "when" to hit the dink.

You have three options:

1. immediately after the ball bounces;
2. when the ball is at the highest point after bouncing; or
3. as the ball is falling after the first bounce and before it bounces again.

Each option for when to hit the ball corresponds roughly with hitting the dink: quickly, medium, or slowly. Generally, it's important to hit the ball sooner rather than later. The reason is that if you take more time to respond, your opponent will have more time to get set up. However, this drill can help you work on mixing up your response times in the right way. If you do it right, mixing up when you respond can really throw off your opponents resulting in them hitting an unforced error, weak dink back to you or an attackable ball.

Dink, Volley, Attack

This is a good drill to help you improve your sense of discernment. The drill practices making good choices while playing at the kitchen line. Since playing at the kitchen line is a regular part of the game and an essential part of competitive and advanced games, I recommend this drill be revisited regularly to keep your senses fresh.

When you're playing at the kitchen (non-volley zone) and you're in the ready position, you have three options for shots: dink, volley, or attack. To refresh your memory from earlier lessons, your shot choice depends a lot on the height of the ball at the point you take your shot and make contact with the ball.

Here are the ideal options for each scenario:

Discernment: ball is below the net, the correct shot is a Dink.

Dink: when the ball bounces in front of you

Volley: when the ball is roughly at the height of the net, but not high enough for you to hit down on the ball towards your opponents feet and still have a high margin of error to ensure the ball goes over the net

Attack: when the ball is much higher than the net so you easily hit down on the ball

Discernment: ball is much higher than the net, the correct shot is an Attack.

Discernment: ball is at your mid-section, the correct shot is a Volley.

towards your opponents feet, to the gap in the middle or angle to the side.

To practice the drill, you and your partner hit back and forth. On each shot focus on making the right choice for each shot: dink, volley, or attack. If you are unsure of the level of the ball, consider other factors like the speed and angle of the ball. If it's at net height but quickly angling upward, it may become attackable by the time you can hit it.

Remember, deciding which shot to make is all about discernment. You don't want to dink an attackable ball. Similarly, you don't want to attack a ball that should be dinked or volleyed, and vice versa. As with most drills, the main advantage of practicing this is creating some brain memory and muscle memory to know to dink when the ball is low, volley when it's mid-height, and attack when it's high.

FOOTWORK DRILLS

Footwork is fundamental to just about every pickleball point you'll play. These drills will help improve your balance and may help you minimize injuries on the court. After all, staying safe is an important skill in any sport.

To know if your footwork needs some work, here are good benchmarks to gauge your movement and technique:

1. If you are not balanced in your ready position.
2. If you are not balanced when hitting the ball.
3. If you are not stopping early when your opponent starts their backswing.
4. If you are moving while hitting (when you should be stopped).
5. If you are reaching to hit the ball (instead of using your feet to get closer to the ball).

One Step Progressions
This is one of the best drills I've encountered to maintain a good balance for your forward movement. Forward movement is something you use in every rally!

Follow these steps:

STEP 1 Hit a forehand from the baseline.

Hit a forehand from the baseline.

One step, get into your transition area ready position.

STEP 2 Take one step in, and stop. Get into your transition area ready position, paddle down in front of you, paddle angle up, weight forward, knees bent.

Another step, maintain your transition area ready position.

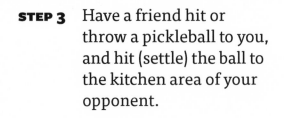

STEP 3 Have a friend hit or throw a pickleball to you, and hit (settle) the ball to the kitchen area of your opponent.

STEP 4   Repeat step 2.

Another step, continue to maintain your transition ready position.

You're now at the kitchen line. Move to your kitchen-ready position.

STEP 5 Repeat Steps 3 and 4 until you reach the kitchen line, and have your drill partner throw you a ball that you can dink, volley or attack.

STEP 6 Repeat Steps 1–6.

This exercise helps to avoid running mindlessly toward the kitchen line. It also helps to improve footwork, reinforce the ready positions and avoid unnecessary reaching for the ball, which can throw you off balance. Slowing down and stopping early will also build up your awareness about each step you take.

I practice this drill with students regularly. Moving to the kitchen is a fundamental piece to every rally you'll play in pickleball. You want to do it correctly. Maintaining good footwork, balance and early preparation as you advance to the kitchen line are some things many players overlook.

Lateral Step vs. Cross-Court
This is one of the few drills that you can actually practice solo. You can also use a wall to hit against. It can also be fun with other players. Since it involves

Solid ready position at kitchen line.

One lateral step to your left.

One lateral step to your right.

moving around, it can also function as a warm-up drill to help get the blood flowing.

To do this, step laterally along the kitchen (non-volley zone) with no cross-stepping. Take a step with your right foot, leave your left foot in place and then move back to your ready position by stepping back with your right foot. For the next step, take a step with your left foot, leave your right foot in place and move back to your ready position by stepping back with your left foot.

The key is avoiding stepping backward or any cross-steps that may throw off your balance, alter your otherwise good swing motion, take too much time to recover and or open up gaps for your opponent to hit. If you have a partner, you can add dinking and volleying back and forth, as you both step laterally along the kitchen line. If you don't have a partner, use a wall and step laterally with your right foot, return to your ready position, step with your left foot, return to your ready position all while dinking and then volleying from 7 feet away from the wall.

TIPS FOR WARMING UP

I can remember one time playing without bothering to warm up and just thinking to myself, "I'll be okay." What happened is that I soon ended up missing three shots, missing the third-shot drop each time. These are shots I should have easily made, and I thought to myself, "I missed those shots only because I didn't take a little time to go through the motions of hitting them in warmups!" It was a great reminder for me. So often, especially at open play sessions you step on the court and some players want to start playing a game immediately. Please resist the temptation and go through your complete warm up routine.

Stretching

Anybody who has played sports before has inevitably learned their lesson on the importance of warming up. In my mind, warming up involves dynamic stretching versus static stretching. In essence, this means to be moving or actively shifting position as you are stretching, not just stretching while completely stationary. One way to do this is to simply walk around the court a few times, the more the better.

What I do with students is to have everyone walk around the courts with high leg lifts. This initial walk around gets out the kinks without risking pulling a muscle. A few minutes of stretching can go a long way in preventing unnecessary injuries.

Practice the Shots

I've learned to practice all the main shots I'll use in a game during my warmup before any important game. Otherwise, there is always a good chance one of the first shots you make is going to be a bad one. One reason for this is muscle memory. It takes our body and mind some time to snap into gear and to have all the right muscles fired up and regain your muscle memory. Better to get rid of that bad shot in a warm up than during a moment that really matters.

Here is the breakdown of our standard warm up routine and some typical warmup shots:

- 20 cross-court dinks from each side
- 20 reflex volleys
- 10 forehand drop shots from the transition area
- 10 backhand drop shots from the transition area
- 10 forehand drives from the baseline
- 10 backhand drives from the baseline
- 10 forehand drop shots from the baseline
- 10 backhand drop shots from the baseline
- 5 overheads from the kitchen line
- 5 practice serves to each side

Once you have practiced these warm-up shots, you feel more confident in starting to play!

Altogether this warm up routine should take about 10 to 20 minutes. In addition to injury prevention, this warmup is designed to trigger muscle and brain memory so that you have already hit most of the shots in the warm-up that you will need in the game.

HEALTH BENEFITS OF PICKLEBALL

Playing pickleball will not necessarily guarantee a miraculous improvement in your physical health. But the evidence suggests it will definitely improve the odds! For starters, a study published on NPR in 2017 indicated that playing pickleball will burn 40% more calories than walking.[4]

In addition to burning more calories than walking, you get many positive effects from producing endorphins while playing. One study showed that those who played at least three times a week saw "improved blood pressure and cardiorespiratory fitness."[5] Many also report improved balance and agility, something important at all age levels.[6]

I have seen these benefits play out in the lives of so many students. My student Terrie shared this about her dramatic physical and mental improvements from playing:

"I had a total spinal fusion in my early '50s. So there are many things that are challenging to do. I am restricted in what I can do. Unfortunately, I had to take eight years off from any strenuous activity because of these orthopedic issues. Playing pickleball gave me confidence in movements.

---

[4] https://www.npr.org/sections/health-shots/2017/10/19/558212306/pickleball-for-all-the-cross-generational-power-of-play
[5] https://www.aarp.org/home-family/friends-family/info-2018/pickleball-health-social-emotional-benefits.html
[6] https://www.courtreserve.com/top-7-health-and-social-benefits-of-pickleball/

Getting exercise, when you cannot get it, it's going to make you feel better, not only physically but emotionally."

My student Carolyn shared this:

"I have seen some players drop some significant weight. I know at least two friends who lost 50 to 60 pounds. Several got back into physical shape as they got into a regular exercise and pickleball routine."

According to the National Institutes of Health, "fewer adults meet guidelines for aerobic physical activity."[7] Many claim a big reason for this is that they don't have activities to do that are enjoyable.[8] As a solution to improving exercise and aerobic activity, the organization recommends pickleball for those over 50. Its studies also mention how the sport maximizes fun while minimizing stress on the joints and excess movement.

The state government of New York invested in pickleball courts in areas of cities with limited access to sports and athletic facilities.[9]

The Parkinson Foundation of Western Pennsylvania cites many benefits of playing pickleball for those struggling with such severe illnesses, such as Parkinson's. One player who has Parkinson's, Andy Leighton, noted that "pickleball is an ideal activity for those with Parkinson's because it occupies your mind and you're also physically active."[10] Andy also observed, "Without pickleball, I would not be in as good of shape."[11]

His wife added, "Pickleball allowed him to stay off meds for about a year or so, and because it keeps him moving, it keeps his symptoms at bay."[12]

---

[7] https://www.ncbi.nlm.nih.gov/pmc/articles/PMC5723370/
[8] https://www.ncbi.nlm.nih.gov/pmc/articles/PMC5723370/
[9] https://philanthropynewyork.org/news/why-pickleball
[11] https://pfwpa.org/services/exercise-lifestyle/parkinsons-pickleball/
[12] Ibid.

My student Carolyn mentioned:

"Pickleball has given self-confidence back to me. It has elevated my sense of confidence, and I feel mentally strong because of it. This feeling comes because I am confident that I am the best player I can be at that moment. This allows me to compete in tournaments."

The Social Side

Pickleball has all of these health benefits, but we haven't even considered how all the social benefits can have a positive impact on health, too!

Loneliness is a phenomenon that is affecting all age groups, and especially older age groups in the United States at greater rates than in the past. For many reasons, people are just left out more often. Pickleball is an emerging method for people to get together in groups and clubs in a very positive way.

One study showed lower rates of depression from regularly participating in pickleball at the tournament level.[13] Many people have also reported how their camaraderie improves over time as they play more pickleball.[14]

---

[13] Ibid.

[14] https://www.aarp.org/home-family/friends-family/info-2018/pickleball-health-social-emotional-benefits.html

ABOUT THE AUTHOR

John is the founder of Callahan Pickleball Academy and is a USAPA/PPR "Certified Pickleball Professional," an IPTPA "Certified Pickleball Teaching Professional," and a 2019 U.S. Open Gold & Silver Medalist.

John has been teaching Pickleball full time, seven days a week, for three years His students include: tennis players, beginners with no athletic background, All-American athletes, and U.S. Open Gold Medal winners. Through his lessons, clinics, camps and events, he's helped thousands improve their game.

John has taught with some of the top coaches and players in the country. He won a Gold medal (and a Silver medal) at the 2019 U.S. Open playing with one of his students.

Currently John teaches pickleball in St. Louis, MO at Dwight Davis Tennis Center in Forest Park and Creve Coeur Racquet Club.

PICKLEBALL NOTES

_____

_____

_____

_____

_____

_____

_____

_____

_____

_____

_____

PICKLEBALL NOTES

_____

_____

_____

_____

_____

_____

_____

_____

_____

_____

_____

_____

PICKLEBALL NOTES

PICKLEBALL NOTES

PICKLEBALL NOTES

_____

_____

_____

_____

_____

_____

_____

_____

_____

_____

_____

_____

PICKLEBALL NOTES

PICKLEBALL NOTES

_____

_____

_____

_____

_____

_____

_____

_____

_____

_____

_____

PICKLEBALL NOTES

PICKLEBALL NOTES

_____

_____

_____

_____

_____

_____

_____

_____

_____

_____

_____

_____

AUTHOR'S NOTES

This book is a collective effort by the following:

Author: John R. Callahan
Writer: Marc Jorgensen
Editor: Drew Robison
Co-editors: Marc Jorgensen, Charlie Cai
Designer: Stephen Tiano
Photographers: Danny Reise, Terry Rolwes, Super Dave Tedoni, and many others who contributed ideas, time and encouragement.

Thank you all!!

John R. Callahan

Made in the USA
Las Vegas, NV
25 February 2021